BRITANNIA

Rowing Alone Across the Atlantic

BRITANNIA : *Rowing*

Alone Across the Atlantic

THE RECORD OF AN ADVENTURE

by John Fairfax

WILLIAM KIMBER
London

ACKNOWLEDGMENTS

I extend my most heartfelt thanks to all who so gladly put their assistance, advice, equipment or facilities at my disposal in connection with this voyage. Without their invaluable cooperation, I would undoubtedly have been incapable of undertaking a venture of this magnitude. To those listed here, and to those whose names are not listed from fault of memory, but whose aid is nevertheless equally appreciated, I am and will remain eternally grateful.

Uffa Fox, for *Britannia*'s beautiful design.

Martin Cowling, for financing the building of *Britannia*.

Clare Lallow, for building *Britannia* so soundly.

My mother, the real heroine of this story, for her patience and forbearance.

Sylvia Cook, for her great help, both before and after, and also for typing this book.

John Stevens, for tracking down and acquiring most of my more technical equipment.

Group Captain Peter Whittingham, O.B.E., M.D., of the Royal Air Force Institute of Aviation Medicine, Aldershot, for advice and equipment for survival at sea.

Ron Bullen of the Serpentine Boat House in Hyde Park, for giving me the freedom of his boats for training.

Malcolm Davies of Calor Gas, Ltd., for supplying fuel for my cooking and water distilling, and designing the apparatus.

Expanded Rubber and Plastics, Ltd., for supplying the Plastazote from which *Britannia*'s buoyancy chambers were built.

Ayling and Son of Putney, for the oars which made the crossing possible.

George Sims, for the sliding seat which went on sliding.

Edwin H. Phelps, for the seat tracks which never jammed.

Matt Wood, for unfailing rowlocks.

L. W. Madaline of the British Red Cross Society, for advice and first-aid supplies.

Archie de Jong of Horlicks, Ltd., for advice on the nutritional problems.

Tom Hanley, for the many excellent photographs taken prior to departure.

Rolex of Geneva, for the outstanding chronometer.

Kelvin Hughes, for servicing and restoring my battered old sextant.

Ronsons, for the lighter which saved my life.

Don Salvador Moret of Gran Hotel Las Caracolas in Las Palmas, for exceeding the hospitality expected of any hotel in helping with my special problems.

Ron Stringer of the Marconi Company, for his tireless energy installing my CH25 Marconi radio in the cramped, hot conditions on board *Britannia* in Las Palmas.

Independent Television News, for its help in Las Palmas and for keeping in radio contact at unearthly hours throughout my journey.

Noel Botham and Jeff White of the *Daily Sketch*, for much slavery in Las Palmas.

Val Schaeffer and the crew of *Camelot*, for towing *Britannia* from Las Palmas to San Agustín throughout the night of January 18, 1969.

Bruce and Myra Pearson of the Marina Motor Inn, Fort Lauderdale, for their kind hospitality and friendship upon my arrival in Florida.

Ken Crutchlow and Su Nadel, for their indefatigable help after my landing.

Peter Learmont 'of the Royal Manhattan Hotel in New York, for the best of British hospitality.

My special gratitude to the captains of all the ships that stopped for me along the way.

Rauf Bulent, Anneke Land, Brian Watkins, Marylyn Walshe, Captain Garrido López—and the many, many other kind individuals who I hope will forgive me for not naming them, as a complete list would fill a book.

Last, but not least, Sylvia's dad and Ian Sanderson, for taking my mind away from it all during relaxing chess evenings.

J.F.

Contents

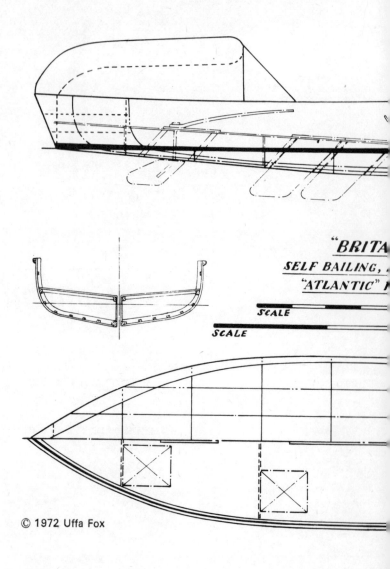

"BRITA

SELF BAILING,

"ATLANTIC"

SCALE

SCALE

© 1972 Uffa Fox

Britannia's lines show a very easily driven hull, essential for the strength of one man, also the self-righting chambers each end that afforded shelter.

The self-bailing deck is seen in the profile sloping down to the foot rest and two daggerboards. The constructional section to

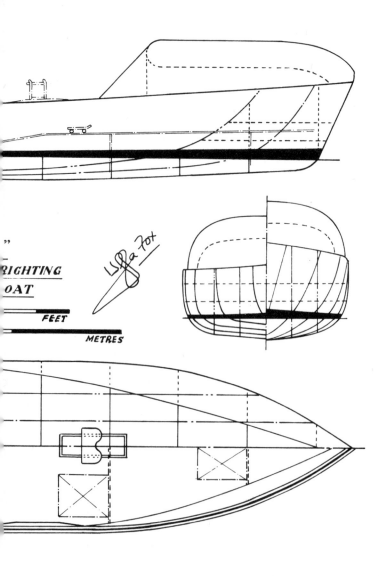

the left shows the ramp down to the centre-line and the self-bailing slots. The lower half of the plan view shows the watertight
hatches, starboard side, for stowing food and gear, only one to
be opened at a time.

TO UFFA FOX,
Grand Old Man of the Sea

Non possono i fulmini, la rabbia de' venti,
la morte, l'amore sviarlo dal mar. . . .

Neither thunder, nor raging winds,
nor death, nor love can turn him from the sea. . . .

FROM *Un Ballo in Maschera*
by Giuseppe Verdi

PART I:

The Plan

1

"Seven! Seven out!*

"Seven! Seven out!" Once more the recollection of those fateful words brought a savage curse to my lips; and the sight of the dark, majestic mass of Buckingham Palace, invoking visions of untold splendors within as it loomed in the mist of that chilly winter's night, did nothing to mitigate my fury. That it was raining and I had been walking for the last half hour toward my little room near Victoria Square did not help either. And I was walking because in a final gesture of grandeur, after losing the last of my £300 at a craps table in the Casino, I had tipped the porter half a crown, quite heedless of the fact that it was my very last coin.

By the very nature of my life I am, of necessity, a gambler.

* An American dice, or craps, term. The number seven wins on the first roll of the dice; at any time after that it loses, and the croupier will call, "Seven out."

In spite of this, formal gambling affords me no delight and is a pastime I slight until desperate—and tonight, and for three nights before, I had been desperate.

It was all very simple, really. A resident of Argentina, I had arrived in England with £300 and the hope of interesting somebody—a newspaper, most likely; otherwise, anybody else—in sponsoring me in my intended attempt to row single-handed across the Atlantic. Not an easy task, since the project would require something in the region of £5,000. Also, although English, I had never been in England before; I had no contacts and no idea how to approach the problem. Quite aside from that, only four men had attempted to row the Atlantic in this century. One two-man crew had succeeded; the other two men had perished. No one had ever tried to row across single-handed. To make matters worse, as far as the newspapers were concerned, the two Englishmen, Johnston and Hoare, who had attempted the row the previous year in a little boat called *Puffin*, were the ones who had been lost. Their boat had only just been found, empty and overturned, with no sign of the occupants.

For nearly two months after my arrival I had walked all over London, introducing myself to dozens of people in my attempt to raise the necessary sponsorship. Unfortunately, the memory of the *Puffin* was too fresh, and the mere mention of my intention was enough for anybody not to wish to be involved with me. Everybody said it was impossible for a single man to row the Atlantic. Confident that it was only a matter of time and perseverance before I would, eventually, find sponsorship, I was equally aware that by then I would probably have no money left on which to live. As no cash was forthcoming whilst my little capital fast dwindled away, I decided to play all on one card. Gambling seemed the quick solution. If I won, my problems would be solved. If I lost—well, I would think about that when it happened. As a fatalist, I firmly believe that nothing bad ever happens without something good to follow. Who is to say, anyway, what is the will of the gods?

Still shivering after my hour-long walk in the rain, I finally tucked myself into bed with the thought that a bench in Hyde Park is not quite the best place to sleep in London during January. My rent being due on the morrow, I fell asleep with the uneasy conviction that I was much better off now that my problem was not that of finding £5,000 for a boat, but that of finding a mere £6 to appease a landlady.

From the first day, in spite of my general dislike of big cities, I had liked London. Why, I discovered the following morning, as, in my somewhat lost and penniless state, I looked into her foggy, cold, unwashed face. They seemed to be everywhere—the most tantalizing, beautiful legs in the world, as scores of miniskirted girls appeared and disappeared, ghostlike, out of and into the mist. The fact that they were probably on their way to a dull, dreary routine in anything-but-romantic little offices did nothing to dispel their charm. To me they were like so many nameless little ships without harbor, and I let my eyes follow them, dreamily, in a strange mixture of happiness and nostalgia.

A sudden screech as a car pulled to a stop just behind me, and a selective string of curses, brought me back to reality with a jolt. Reality in the shape of my landlady and her toothless grin, which had all but spoiled my breakfast whilst she politely but firmly declined to share my views on the irrelevance of a week's rent as compared with the greatness to come. The poor thing all too obviously lacked vision, and I was further handicapped by a natural weakness of mine, a frustrating inability to switch on any charm whatsoever when confronted with a sour old goat.

One battle lost, another began; then another, and another, until by midafternoon I had lost count. Apparently there was no need for a man of my varied talents in London.

The time to pick and choose among jobs was clearly passing—but, catering being an unknown field of activity in my experience, I decided to explore what possibilities it held for me. Accordingly, I walked into a catering employment agency—where, having previously decided that, since I was new to the business, whether I started from the top or from the bottom was a matter of academic irrelevance, I announced myself available for the post of maître d'hôtel. There was no doubt in my mind about my capability of handling the job. Alas, bureaucracy, in the shape of the pale, fat, balding little man facing me across the desk, was not prepared to give me the opportunity. His curiosity was limitless, and he wanted to know all about my qualifications, previous experience, what kind of working papers I had, who had been my last employer, why I had left my last job, why . . . Why? What? Where? Questions and more questions. All day I had seen my very best intentions snubbed by questions, and this time I couldn't take it any more—so I told him.

"My last job?" I said, looking straight into his eyes and keeping a deadpan expression. "Oh, that was last year—give or take a few months. I worked as administrator on a mink farm in Argentina. I was given full authority to overhaul the place, get things going, liven it up. Know what I mean? The farm was losing money, and I was supposed to find out why and change that. Well, the trouble was that when I got the job the old administrator was still there, and until they found a way of getting rid of him, I was provisionally assigned the job of keeping an eye not on the minks, but on the pigs. They had a small pig farm on the side. I don't suppose you know anything about pigs?"

I smiled and, before he could get a word in, went on (I was beginning to enjoy myself), "Well, neither did I. That was rather a mistake, 'cause most of the sows were pregnant, and I fed them with raw potatoes; you are not supposed to feed pigs with raw potatoes, see: it's—er—apparently poisonous; so most of them died, and—well—I was taken away from the pigs and switched my attention to ridding the fields of weeds. Now, the best way of doing that is by fire. If not the best, at least the quickest, and anyway, that was the way I decided to go about it. Everything was going fine till, unfortunately, the wind started blowing from the wrong direction and the fire got somewhat out of hand when a few sparks flew onto the wrong fields. It was harvest time, and I am not sure what the stuff was—wheat, I think—but in any case, it burned spectacularly. They told me the glow could be seen for miles. It must have been beautiful. I was far too busy to appreciate it myself, but . . . They still remember me in those parts. They call me Nero—affectionately, of course. And that was my last job. You want me to tell you why I left it?"

It was definitely not one of my days. For a change I had told the honest truth, and all I got for it was the kind of uneducated remarks one usually associates with troopers.

My next agency also dealt with catering. I walked out of it as a dishwasher—or rather, a prospective dishwasher.

With a French name, a Dutch owner, a Turkish manager, an English chef, a Yugoslav waiter, a Russian singer and last, but not least, myself as dishwasher, the Pierrot Gourmand was a little restaurant with an atmosphere all of its own. The kitchen was by far the most popular place. There, presided over by our manager, Rauf Bulent, a most extraordinary character—ex-millionaire, ex-archaeologist, ex-brother-in-law of the late King Farouk and a professor of English literature; in other words, a man who knew how to live—we used to sing, laugh, drink, play cards and chat away the problems of the world. Mrs. Anneke Land, our charming boss, who lived upstairs, thought we were a funny bunch, and a rather inept one at that. All the same, whenever she came to the kitchen, which was almost every night, regardless of her mood she would eventually accept a glass of her own excellent wine, or maybe two, and cheer up to the fact that life, whenever possible, ought to be enjoyed rather than endured. Somehow, in spite of our joint efforts, the Pierrot Gourmand consistently lost money, and after three months or so, it was unanimously decided it would be best if we all handed in our resignations. Inevitably, with our departure, the Pierrot Gourmand, as such, ceased to exist.

The Pierrot was open only at night, and that suited me admirably, leaving me free to go about my business during the morning and most of the afternoon. By then I was more than convinced that rowing across the Atlantic in itself would be peanuts compared with my struggle against humanity. It was all the more painful to me as, until then, I had apparently been living under the illusion that provided I believed in and really cared about something, I could even persuade the Devil to support virtue. But if the foundations of my morale were shaken, they did not crack.

My first lucky break came when I remembered the name of the London correspondent of an Argentine daily paper. A few inquiries led me to the External Services of the BBC at Bush House. Tall, gray-haired, distinguished-looking, George Marin was one of the nicest persons I had met in London.

"What you need," he said, "is somebody to back you up, a name with prestige in the maritime and sailing world."

As if I didn't know! For months now I had been running in a vicious circle, starting with naught and ending with naught.

"We will raise the money if you can show us your boat."

"We will build your boat if you can show us the money."

How to get one without the other, that was the question, and we thoughtfully pondered it—or rather, he did, because to concentrate in the cafeterias around the BBC was obviously a matter of practice. For me, with my starboard peripheral vision covering the possibilities of a luscious blonde and my port ear tingling with the silly giggles of another, pretending to sip inspiration from a cup of cold tea was a sad and frustrating affair.

However, George rose to the occasion by finally suggesting that, with or without money, before a boat could be built

I had to have a design for it, and for that he said, "Uffa Fox is the best person I can think of. He is a grand old man, undoubtedly one of the best yacht designers in England, if not the world. He is also Prince Philip's yachting companion and a foremost authority on anything to do with the sea. If he agrees to design your boat, you have half the battle won."

Uffa Fox? The name rang a bell and I remembered, probably from some magazine or other. He was apparently one of the most lovable, eccentric old salts ever to rig a sail. Married about eleven years, he had never, it was said, held a conversation with his French wife, Yvonne, and was quoted as freely admitting, "She doesn't speak English and I don't speak French. You eat, drink and sleep with your wife, so what is there to talk about?"

A lover of life, a lover of the sea, he seemed to have, at the age of sixty-nine, the fire and vigor of a man of only half his years, and the tales George had heard about his unusual and unpredictable behavior gave me a glimmer of hope. Apparently they still talk about a lecture he gave to the Royal Temple Yacht Club at Ramsgate. Warming to his theme, and never one to stand on ceremony, he had loosened his tie and removed his shoes, while liberally punctuating his lecture with salty asides, to the slight embarrassment of some of the ladies in the audience. According to one girl: "He was in a jolly good mood. I learnt little about sailing, but in other respects certain neglects in my education have been rectified."

Clearly a man after my own heart. George told me I would probably be able to talk to him at the *Daily Express* Boat Show at Earls Court, and so I did. As was to be expected, he was dispensing advice to a crowd of boat lovers on one of the technical stands. I wanted to talk to him alone so hung about for a while, summing him up. He was sitting behind a desk but might as well, for all the difference it made in his appearance, have been standing at the tiller of a sloop braving a Force 8 gale. His hair, as ruffled and colored as the stormy waters of the North Atlantic, shaded incredibly bushy eyebrows, from under which, and above a ridiculously small pair of glasses straddled halfway down his nose, peered the sparkling, mischievous blue eyes of a naughty little boy rejoicing at his last prank. To beat around the bush with a man like Uffa would have been a serious mistake; so the moment he was left alone, I introduced myself and told him straightaway that I had the intention of attempting to become the first man to row the Atlantic single-handed, had come far to do it, had no money and no boat, and would he help? How I went about it I cannot remember, but I do remember the general feeling of dry emptiness, with the tingling of cold sweat somewhere along my back, as I finished and braced myself for the inevitable question I knew would come, why did I want to do it? A question I would not, could not, answer. Not then or there.

With a tinge of scorn which set my blood on fire, he asked, "Row the Atlantic single-handed, eh? And what on earth makes you think you can do it, my boy?"

Gripping the edge of the table so hard it hurt, I leaned forward and told him, "Mr. Fox, I don't need the earth to tell me what I can do. I *know*."

He frowned, and for a second or two, as he stared at me without batting an eyelid, a glimmer of ice replaced the naughty sparkle in his eyes and I had a glimpse, behind the benevolent façade, of the steel the man was made of. The kind that can be only broken, never bent. A second or two and the flicker of mischievous amusement reappeared, with a huge smile and a sea of wrinkles in the weather-beaten face. He slammed his fist on the table and said, "Right! I know exactly what kind of boat you will need, and I will design her for you."

2

Uffa Fox kept his promise. On March 20, 1967, from France (where he was staying), I received the following letter:

My dear Jan,

Enclosed is the arrangement plan for your boat to row across the Atlantic. She is 24 ft. waterline—25 ft. overall—4 ft. 9 beam —displacement 1,860 lbs. (hull and gear: 860 lbs.—food, stores and clothing: 1,000 lbs.).

There is an inflated rubber self-righting chamber 7 ft. long each end and under this you can rest and sleep cosy and comfortably.

Her line of flotation is marked and you will note that while the bow is in the water the stern just kisses the water aft.

Above this the double line shows the deck, and forward this is 12″ above the waterline and 9″ at your sliding seat level and from there it runs down steeply to 3″ above the waterline where your stretchers are situated.

Aft this deck is 8″ above the waterline and runs down to 3″ above the waterline at the stretchers. So all the water shipped will run out through any of the four slots, but especially the two amidships which tells you that you have a self-bailing and a self-righting lifeboat.

Underneath the deck there are five watertight bulkheads athwartships and one running the full length on the centreline, therefore your boat is divided into twelve watertight compartments in which you can stow all your gear neat and tidily out of the way and out of any water.

The openings marked with a Saint Andrew Cross are watertight hatches into these compartments, and the reason the two middle ones are out to one side is to keep them clear of any water running down through the centre and out of the slots, for this deck rakes up on either side in the form of a flat "V."

I have given you a sliding seat with 16″ of movement and you will note that the rowlocks are square such as used in racing, as this will save you a great deal of strain as it means that your oar is held square to its work by the rowlock and that when you swing the blades forward and they are feathered they will remain flat to the water by themselves.

With normal round rowlocks and round oars you have to grip them firmly to hold them in their correct position square to the work or flat when the blades are swung forward, so they will cut through any unbroken water cleanly.

Your seat is 7″ above your heels and the bottom of the rowlock 9″ above your seat.

There are four slots through the boat all 12″ wide and you can put a dagger board down any one of these four and also the rudder can go down the after one.

As you will only have one dagger board and one rudder, two of these slots will always be opened to let water shipped down through.

There is 2 ft. of clearance between the under side of the self-righting chambers and the deck which is the minimum you can have for laying under.

I would like you to look through all of this and think it over carefully, and at the same time remember that during the war I designed all the Airborne Lifeboats that brought so many of our gallant airmen home safely from the Bay of Biscay, Heligoland, etc. . . . etc. . . . in even winter gales, and this is a small edition of these Airborne Lifeboats.

We could shorten her down to 20 ft., but I believe you will be glad of this size boat when chasing away down the face of the great Atlantic grey Beards.

The best builder would be: Clare Lallow of Cowes, but he is sure to be snowed under with work this time of the year, and I wonder if you can approach him and ask him to suggest someone else if he cannot build.

Best wishes,

> Yours sincerely,
> UFFA FOX

Enclosed were detailed blueprints and a sketch of what the boat would eventually look like.

So now I had my design and one of the best names in the yachting world behind me. I had done it! It was a time for celebration!

As it happened, the kitchen of the Pierrot Gourmand was livelier than usual that night—so much so that, in trying to match the exuberance of my spirits with the effervescence of the champagne, I completely forgot that I could not cross the Atlantic on a sheet of paper. Thus, with the end of the last bottle, began the most depressing year of my existence.

A lifetime of adventurous ups and downs should have taught me to beware if things suddenly turn out, or appear, too easy, but somehow I never do. Mind you, a glass of wine, a beautiful girl and "everything's going my way." Even at its worst, my luck has seldom been so bad that I have been unable to indulge in such simple tastes. All the same, to keep head and shoulders soaring in the company of eagles whilst feet and ankles shuffle in the mud calls for some stretching. Sooner or later, something is bound to give.

"The best way of doing things," I was told, "is to get in touch with a literary agency and let *them*, on the strength of the book you will write about your adventure, raise the necessary capital for the building of the boat."

This I did. It was the first step toward the Atlantic.

My disillusionment came gradually. At the beginning of our contract I was full of high hopes, and as the agency's advance of £250 coincided with my leaving the Pierrot Gourmand, I decided to put the money to good use and take my revenge on the casinos.

This may sound foolish, and I agree that it usually is. However, one must not forget that I am, by profession, an adventurer. A rough life perhaps, but also, if successful, highly rewarding. It matters little if, along the line, now and then one finds oneself doing a spell as a stevedore, canal digger, interpreter, bodyguard, nightclub photographer or—why not?—dishwasher. An overall education is always useful, and as a good friend of mine used to say, "There is no better way for a young fellow who wants to see the best of both worlds than sleeping with a countess in the morning and a streetwalker at night."

But now I found myself in a dilemma. To row a boat across the Atlantic calls for something more than a knowledge of navigation and survival at sea. First and foremost, one has to be fit. Important as it is, it would do me no good to know my stars if I lacked the stamina to pull on the oars and follow them, hour after hour, day after day, for months.

My original plan, which was to row from Newfoundland to England, called for a strict timetable. The latest I could start was June, three months away. According to the Pilot Charts, I could then hope to have about three months of fairly steady westerly winds; after that, the winds would become more and more variable, increasingly changing into easterlies and northeasterlies. To start from scratch and be ready in three months' time was, I realize now, a forlorn hope, but I had to try or lose the season, with the implication of having to wait for the next—that is to say, June 1968. An unbearable thought.

One thing was clear: I had to start training in earnest, and that would be a full-time job. Proper training means not only plenty of exercise but plenty of food and rest as well. To have one without the other is defeating the purpose. Also, I had to find suitable suppliers for the best equipment and stores I could gather. To do this and work at the same time was clearly out of the question, yet training and traveling around would be an expensive business. The £ 180-odd I had left from my advance, after settling my few debts, was not likely to last long.

There was no likelihood of getting a further advance. So I went back to the craps table, watching the dice roll, determined to get my own back. Every night I worked at it for about two hours—hating every minute, as it was a matter not of pleasure but of necessity. The way I see it there are only two ways to gamble: big, or not at all. Since I was unable to follow either, I had to go for the exception—that is to say, to play very carefully, never allowing myself to lose more than a small set amount and always, *always* leaving when on a winning run. It takes a lot of discipline and all the fun out of it, but with a moderate amount of luck, it is possible in this way to win consistently enough to stay out of the red for a while. I contented myself with winning an average of £5 a night, which was not bad.

My training comprised about a couple of miles' running every morning, two hours' weight lifting and swimming at the YMCA and some three or four hours' rowing on the Serpentine. For the information of those who have not yet had the privilege of visiting England, the Serpentine is a small lake, five-eighths of a mile long, in Hyde Park, London. In spite of the years I had spent at sea, my rowing experience at the time was limited to the odd comings and goings in dinghys or similar boats, mainly from ship to shore. I made no bones about it, and I had the slight feeling that a lot of people found the fact hard to swallow that the man who planned to row across the Atlantic single-handed was bridging the gap in his rowing experience by splashing up and down a pond, between ducks and geese, in a public park in the middle of London. A few newspapers took the opportunity to pull my leg, and I cannot really blame them for that. It was precisely because of its location I found training on the Serpentine extremely convenient; and after all, I wanted exercise, and I can assure anyone who has not tried it that rowing flat out in still water, nonstop, for a couple of hours is plenty. The same goes for my rowing technique, which according to the purists was, and is, nonexistent—to which all I can say is "So what?" Knowing my limitations, I know perfectly well that I will never make Henley, but then, who wants to? I hate rowing, anyway.

Why row across the Atlantic, then? Because, with a bit of know-how, almost anybody can sail, but I was after a battle against nature at its most primitive and raw. For fifteen years I had dreamed about it, since reading the tremendous saga of two Norwegians, George Harbo and Frank Samuelson, who had seemingly achieved the impossible.

They had become the first men ever to cross the Atlantic Ocean in a tiny boat with no other means of propulsion than oars. What an awesome ordeal they had lived through! But their reward had been the satisfaction of getting out of it alive, of having won, by sheer determination, willpower, endurance, against all the odds, proving once more what man can do, the vital flame that burns in him that enabled him to become a man in the first place, through the ages and before, when there was nothing! I had kept the account of their amazing journey under my pillow, reading and rereading it, my boyish imagination lit by a fury of sparks which burned and glowed till I was all but consumed in its fire. An ideal was born. One day I too would row the Atlantic. But I would do it alone. To those who may feel inclined to ask, "To what purpose?" (to them, surely, the whole venture of rowing across the Atlantic was a useless exercise to begin with), I have no answer, and don't suppose I ever will have, except that it mattered to me, and if that makes me selfish, then I am selfish. What price has life, anyway? No two persons will ever give the same value to their own or to other people's lives. Personally, I have always considered life to be worthless unless I could do with it what I wanted and felt I had to do.

Rowing up and down the Serpentine was tremendously boring—but it gave me an inkling of what it would be like out there, with nothing but sky and water to stare at, for months on end. On sunny days, surrounded by cheerful couples and boatloads of kids happily bumping into one another, I had difficulty in concentrating on what I was doing. On others, cold, windy and gray, I found myself almost alone. It was these days I preferred. My mind would then retreat into itself, tentatively tasting the loneliness to come, the monotony, the hardships—and liking it. Watching the blades go in and out, in, out, constantly, steadily pushing the boat along, *was* boring; but at the same time, there seemed to be a determined, single-minded, tireless sense of purpose in it.

3

June 1967 came and went. By then all I had succeeded in doing was to become as fit as I was ever likely to be. Of sponsors there were no signs—and by the look of things, there never would be. In desperation, I put an advertisement in the Personal column of *The Times*, briefly stating my intention of rowing across the Atlantic single-handed in a boat designed by Uffa Fox. Was there anybody interested in helping in any way?

In answer I received six letters. Three from cranks; one from a student who was willing to help in building the boat; one from the Lynch family of Potters Bar (a charming letter full of encouragement and best wishes, together with a check for £1) and one from a girl who said she thought it was a magnificent thing for me to do and offered to help in all possible ways during her free time as a secretary.

My intention had been to interest some large company in

financing the whole project in return for publicity. I had never expected private persons to send money with their best wishes in lieu of help, and I was so touched by it that I had that check for £1 framed and have, since then, kept it among my few treasured possessions. As for the girl—Sylvia Cook was her name, and I phoned her up and arranged an appointment for that very same day. She proved to be a charming girl, a keen rower herself. I was definitely not her type, nor she mine, but in spite of this we liked each other, and after a while I forgot all the others and went out exclusively with her. As far as 1967 was concerned, she was the only bright light in my life.

Things went from bad to worse, and to save money, I moved from my bed-sitting room to her flat in Earls Court, which she shared with three or four other girls. We celebrated the end of the old year in high spirits, and faced the new one with the knowledge that nothing could possibly get worse. It did.

When, after seven months, my lucky run in the casinos began to show signs of turning sour, I was most reluctant to admit that all good things must, eventually, come to an end. Finally my losses, albeit small, became so frequent that gambling was no longer a paying proposition and I had to quit. What now?

Those who know me will say that by no stretch of the imagination can I be called a hard worker—which is absolutely true. Other than during the course of an adventure, I dislike, in fact positively loathe, work. Furthermore, as far as my hands are concerned, again unless I am alone and *have* to do it, I am the first to admit that I cannot even nail four planks of wood into a box without making a mess of it. Since my discovery, early in life, that most people, given a chance to show off their abilities, will seldom fail to exploit the opportunity, I have had a comparatively easy life as the traditional ham-fisted moron caricatured in comic strips. Once, during a hunting trip with a friend, I was outclassed to the extent that

I ended up having to do everything myself, from pitching the tent, setting traps and lighting the fire to even cooking—but that, as they say, is another story. What I mean is that I would much rather use my head than my hands, and the reason for such a long preamble is to make this inclination of mine crystal clear: that I will always try a thousand and one schemes before actually submitting to the sad necessity of grabbing a hammer or a shovel. This time, however, my native inventiveness seemed to have deserted me, leaving me in a tangle of despondency.

After a year and a half in England, apart from Uffa Fox's design I was no nearer my goal than I had ever been; if anything, my prospects of succeeding had never looked gloomier. Not only that, but I felt hurt and disillusioned. In Argentina there had been plenty of sponsors ready to finance me. It had been only through my romantic ideas of patriotism that I had rejected their offers. "If I ever row the Atlantic," I had told them, "it will have to be in an English-built boat flying the Union Jack, or not at all."

For someone who was supposed to be a cool, hardheaded adventurer, I had indeed behaved like a fool and was, dimly, beginning to realize the fact. Why, if nobody was interested, then it was time for me to go back to my earlier life in the Caribbean, where I knew, from previous experience, I would find adventures galore, women and money, life or death, there to be had as I chose! I was tempted, how sorely tempted! But to do that would have been to admit defeat; to make a total, unconditional surrender of my principles— which, damned few as they were, good or bad, sensible or not, were all I had, and without them I would no longer be myself, whatever that was. What would life be worth then? Even to think of giving up would have made me unfit to row the Atlantic!

So I persevered, in an uphill struggle during which I had to swallow my pride so many times I began to seethe with frustrated rage—which was good, as the more I was stung by exasperation, the greater became my resolve to succeed. During these months, Sylvia showed terrific understanding; and as it cannot have been easy to put up with my moods— which she did, apart from helping me in many other ways—I think she deserves all the praise as far as this part of my venture is concerned. Eventually, when my patience was about to run out and I was beginning to contemplate the undertaking of some really drastic measures to get what I needed, there was a break in the clouds through which appeared a glimmer of hope.

By then I had another agent, John Austin, who, together with his partner, John Stevens, had been trying to get my project off the ground by raising the necessary capital to start construction on the boat. It was John Stevens, a freelance do-it-all, who mentioned the idea to a Yorkshire businessman whilst discussing the possibilities of starting a publicity campaign for fried chicken, or something. Martin Cowling was the businessman—who, after discussing it with Morag, his wife, decided it might be fun to be involved in a project like mine instead of just reading about it in the papers. He was willing to finance the boat provided, he said, I was able to convince him not only of the feasibility of my venture but that I was capable of carrying it out. Or, to put it bluntly, he was not prepared to help a lunatic forfeit his life for a bit of cheap glory, at his expense. Fair enough; all I needed was somebody with an open mind and a measure of that spirit of adventure once so prevalent in this little island.

He came to London, and we met for lunch somewhere in Fleet Street. We seemed to get along from the word go, and the deal was sealed. Again it was too late for me to start from Newfoundland; but knowing this, I had chosen an alternative course: the Canary Islands to Florida. It was a much longer route—almost twice as long as the one followed by those who had previously undertaken to row across the Atlantic. Since I had to *row*, not sail, across, the disadvantage was obvious, but so was the challenge. After all, nobody had ever tried to row that way, and I could become not only the first person to row the Atlantic single-handed, but the first to do it from east to west.

With Martin's financial support, the building of *Britannia*, as I had chosen to name the boat, began immediately. At the request of Uffa Fox, who wanted to keep an eye on the construction, we chose a boatyard on the Isle of Wight, and the task was undertaken by Clare Lallow, who, together with Wilf Souter, was considered to be one of the best boatbuilders in England.

We still had problems, however. Martin had agreed to finance the boat, nothing else. The rest of the money we had to find ourselves. John Stevens took over the task of gathering the necessary equipment and stores, while John Austin set about selling the story of the forthcoming journey to a newspaper. As for me, I had to start training all over again while sorting out the survival logistics created by the choice of a new route. This time, however, even though I was still penniless, the gods decided once again to smile upon me, and with my return to their favor, everything took on a definite golden outlook.

Ron Bullen, the boathouse manager in Hyde Park, not only greeted me back but, after I told him that although I now would soon have a boat, I could not afford to row on the lake every day, nor as many hours as I would have liked, because I still had no money, he dismissed my concern with a hearty laugh. "Don't you worry about anything, John," he told me. "You may come here and row as often and for as many hours as you wish. Compliments of the house. It's the least we can do for you." Ron's generosity, at a time when I needed it most, was extended to letting me pick his best boats and oars. It is thanks to him, and for that matter the help of everybody else at the boathouse, that I was able to train regularly, and for this I was, and always will be, very grateful. Thank you, Ron; I needed your help more than you will ever know.

As for Sylvia, she not only fed me as if I were a prizefighter but, by digging into her savings, allowed me to train the whole day—then, late into the night, wrote letters, gathered information and kept some semblance of order in rapidly growing files.

With everybody's help, my project soon began to take shape. It must not be forgotten that while the responsibility for failure or success in every venture of this nature will ultimately rest upon the members or member of the expedition, it is only through the goodwill and cooperation of umpteen individuals and organizations that it can be launched. It is only thanks to their dedicated endeavors, which seldom see the limelight, that the final effort is made possible.

The main problem dealt, naturally enough, with survival. In my case, however, survival was not only a matter of staying alive but of being as fit and healthy as could be throughout the journey—which, depending on weather conditions, I figured would take between three and four months. For this I would need water and food in vast quantities; yet the amount of deadweight I could carry was strictly limited by *Britannia*'s size and design, as well as by my own ability to row her along. Ideally, this weight should not have exceeded one thousand pounds, including myself. This may sound a lot; but in practice, once I finished ticking off a preliminary list, the supplies and equipment I considered minimum requirements more than doubled the original estimate. Fifty gallons of water—which, at the rate of half a gallon per day, would last three months—alone topped five hundred pounds. In the tropical conditions in which I would find myself, half a gallon per day would be, according to the experts, totally inadequate. Group Captain Peter Whittingham, O.B.E., M.D., R.A.F., Senior Specialist in Aviation Physiology, Royal Air Force Institute of Aviation Medicine, was alone inclined to think that it might just do, provided I rowed at night only. Even so, fifty gallons allowed no safety margin, as I could not possibly guarantee to finish in three months.

The answer was to find a means of making my own drinking water, not only fast but efficiently and involving the least possible work and fewest possible complications. The most reasonable way seemed to be that of boiling seawater. I took the problem to Malcolm Davies of Calor Gas, who said he would give it to the lab boys and see what they came up with. Eventually, Calor Gas's geniuses produced what turned out to be the perfect solution: a pressure cooker and condenser which, connected by a hose, would enable me to distill half a gallon of seawater in five hours. Calor Gas would provide me with enough fuel to maintain my drinking-water requirements throughout the trip, as well as all that I would need for cooking.

Food was another major source of headaches. It had to be light, easy to cook and stow, varied and, most important, of high caloric content. Dehydrated rations seemed to be the solution, and Archie de Jong, a development physicist working with Horlicks, was the man to approach. What Archie did not know about the nutrition requirements for an expedition at sea, to the poles, across deserts or up mountains was not worth knowing. What is more, he was always willing to cooperate, taking one's interests to heart as if they were his own. He suggested a perfectly balanced daily diet, which would fulfill all my needs—except one: variety. Saying that I did not care as long as it was food was *my* mistake. Actually, lightness being my main concern, there was little I could choose from; but in all fairness to Archie (considering what I will have to say about it later on!), he did warn me I would probably end by hating his guts. Not at all, Archie, not at all—only your food!

Another problem, essential for the story to be sold to a newspaper, was communications. Somehow I had to find a way to be in touch with London throughout the journey. The technical difficulties were enormous, as in spite of her sophistication, *Britannia* was, after all, an open rowboat. I needed a two-way radio, capable of receiving and transmitting voice across a range of at least three thousand miles. It had to be compact, light, rugged and capable of operating with a twelve-volt car battery, which would have to be recharged with a generator. Marconi of Canada had one—the CH25 transceiver—that was ideal, having been specially designed to operate from lorries. It had the incredible range of five thousand nautical miles—and, alas, the even more incredible price of £1,200. Fortunately, Marconi's technicians assured us that they could install the whole shebang and make it operational, and the *Daily Sketch,* sold on the idea of exclusive rights to publish my messages during the crossing, advanced enough money to pay for the radio.

A Honda generator seemed, for size and reliability, to be the best available on the market, but John Stevens shopped around a bit and came up with another even better for our purposes. For one thing, it was English-made; and then, if slightly bulkier, it had such a look of simplicity that I figured if something went wrong even I could handle it. For those who may be interested, it was a Conyers type D 450, and it turned out to be such an excellent piece of machinery that I would not dream of using any other.

For emergencies, Burndept Electronics provided a SARBE (Search and Rescue Beacon Equipment) radio beacon. This is a little gadget that every yacht that goes to sea should carry, as it would not only ensure the safety of those on board but, and to my mind far more relevant, minimize the work and risk of would-be rescuers. Regardless of how many times it happens, few people seem to appreciate the enormous difficulty of finding a small disabled boat at sea. The SARBE is not only comparatively cheap but so small it can be attached to a life jacket. Battery-charged, it will automatically send a signal on two fixed international distress frequencies which will be picked up by any airplane or ship within a two-hundred-mile radius—after which, guided by the beacon, they will be able to home in straight to the disabled vessel. Furthermore, should the rescue party arrive in, say, a helicopter, the SARBE can be used as a walkie-talkie. Surely anyone who goes to sea for his own pleasure, regardless of what he may think his life is worth, ought to consider himself duty-bound to help those who may be called upon to help him at the risk of *their* lives?

So it went, every day bringing a different puzzle to be solved, a fresh difficulty to surmount. There seemed to be no end to it; but as we plodded on, discarding one thing, trying another, never accepting no as a final answer, a fine, clear picture began to emerge, showing that with goodwill and determination, all things are possible.

Britannia was ready to be launched on December 16. Rain was pouring down. The wind swept the Solent with gale force, and we were just in time to see the press hovercraft zoom in. As it was impossible to launch *Britannia* in such appalling weather, the event was postponed for an hour. By eleven o'clock the wind had died down, and although it was still raining, it was decided to go ahead.

Uffa Fox arrived, all wrapped up in sweaters and a huge yellow oilskin. Having suffered a stroke a few weeks before, he was not supposed to have been there at all; but doctor's orders notwithstanding, it would have probably taken a regiment to keep the grand old man away. He seemed to be the happiest person around. His piercing, sparkling blue eyes taking in the slightest detail, the first thing he did was bawl me off for stowing the oars the wrong way round. "Most unseamanlike, John, most unseamanlike! Don't you know better?"

Britannia looked beautiful in her glistening coat of fluorescent orange paint—but while still in dry dock, also huge and unwieldy. I had never rowed in her before, and I felt so nervous in my fear of making an ass of myself in front of everybody, I hardly knew which end was what. For the first time in my life I found myself the focus of attention for over a dozen reporters, asking silly questions all at the same time and hastily scribbling down even more stupid answers. Television cameras whirred, bulbs flashed, the rain kept pouring down and everybody got in everybody's way.

Finally some semblance of order prevailed, and Sylvia and Morag jointly raised the champagne bottle.

"We name this ship *Britannia*. Good luck to her and those who sail in her."

(They were a bit nervous too, and fumbled their lines somewhat. Fancy anyone calling *Britannia* a ship!)

Then they let the bottle go against her bows. Nothing happened.

"Try again girls—harder this time!" said Mr. Lallow.

Nothing.

"Once more, for Christ's sake. Give it to her!"

With the third try the bottle shattered with a crash, showering glass and champagne all over them, and *Britannia*, with me on board, slipped into the water as gracefully as a swan.

In my haste to man the oars, before *Britannia* could be swept under the pier, I fixed the oars and locked the gates with the rowlocks swinging the wrong way round and noticed, with horror, only after the first stroke. Talk about seamanship! What would Uffa say now? Thank God, the old man was busy getting himself into another boat, and I hoped no one else would see the difference. To put things right I would have to ship the oars, unlock the gates, swing the rowlocks into the proper position . . . Out of the question! To make matters worse, I had never before used a sliding seat. And for some reason, nobody had fixed buttons on the oars— how could I have missed *that*?—with the result that they kept skidding toward the water.

Feeling like the world's greatest idiot, I continued to splash about for the benefit of the press and all concerned, looking, as Sylvia gracefully mentioned later, "like a duck out of water." Compared with what Uffa had to say, it was a most charitable comment.

A masterpiece of workmanship and design, *Britannia* was not only beautiful—she was superb. During trials she proved that if capsized, she would right herself in two seconds flat. Swamped, she was bone-dry in half a minute, the water sluicing down the self-bailing slots almost as fast as the eye could follow. Easy to handle, she was a pleasure to row. As for her stability, it was so great two men could stand on a gunwale and she would only tilt over a few inches even when on ballast. Absolutely marvelous! I felt sure I could take such a boat to hell and back without either of us being the worse for it.

All that was left now was to gather the equipment together, ship her to the Canary Islands and . . . money, money. How I longed for the day when I would be on my own in the middle of the ocean without having to worry about where the next penny would come from. In these last few days we were absolutely flooded with bills, as we had left till the last moment buying all the things we had hoped, unsuccessfully, to get free. Luckily, Martin came to the rescue by dipping his hands into his pockets for more than he had originally bargained for.

Britannia was shipped free of charge, as deck cargo, on the *Aragon,* Royal Mail Lines. Sylvia and I, together with John Stevens and his wife, Margaret, flew over a few days later, arriving in Las Palmas in time to receive *Britannia.* To make things as cheap as possible, we went on a two-week package tour. We were joined a day later by Noel Botham and Jeff White, reporter and photographer assigned to cover the venture by the *Daily Sketch.* Shortly afterward my mother flew in from Argentina; and from England Martin and Morag, two cameramen from Independent Television News and a Marconi technician, Ron Stringer, further swelled our group.

We made our headquarters the Hotel Las Caracolas in Las Palmas.

My mother arrived, after an extremely long and tiring flight, at a most unearthly hour of the morning, to be met at Las Palmas airport by what I was afraid would be an overpowering reception committee of four or five strangers and myself. I need not have worried. She was so overcome by our first meeting in over two years, intermingled with the thought that it would probably be our last for another year, that she seemed to have only the vaguest idea of what was going on. It was a wonderful reunion, and in spite of feeling rather like the prodigal son (I had left Argentina telling her I would be back in six months, having rowed across the Atlantic), I was so happy to see her that I felt a huge lump in my own throat. We drove back to the hotel enthusiastically chattering the nonstop trivia of long-lost friends and went to bed, to restart the day at a more civilized hour.

My intention had been to relax and sunbathe on the beach all day long—with, possibly, occasional visits to the Royal Nautical Club, where *Britannia* was berthed, to see how things were going with her. Unfortunately, I, the only Spanish-speaking member of our party, was soon nominated official interpreter and found myself dashing up and down wherever my services happened to be required—which was everywhere except the beach. What was hard to believe was the amount of equipment still not organized. It is very easy and absolutely reasonable for an outsider to say, "Surely you had lists of everything," but that was only the start of the problem. From my point of view, much of the equipment I did have I never saw until it was uncrated in Las Palmas, which meant it was then, and only then, that I could have a really good look at things to see which parts looked especially vulnerable, what tools I would need, what screws or nails might be necessary, et cetera. Also, I had reckoned that a good many items would be considerably less expensive in the Canaries. Add to this the many helpful suggestions that came flooding in, both from members of our party and from the Spaniards, such as clothes-pegs (!?) and bellows(!?), and you have some idea of the length of the shopping list.

It was agreed that the best plan of attack would be to split up our party into pairs and delegate certain items from the list to each couple. Besides the actual shopping (itself a major undertaking more than trebly complicated by the shoppers' lack of Spanish), further boat trials had to be made, photographs taken, *Britannia's* keel given a new coat of antifouling paint, arrangements made for boiling my water supply and everything thoroughly checked and tested. I must admit that the result of all this was that not one member of our group had his dream holiday lolling around in sunny Las Palmas; in fact, Morag said she had never worked so hard in all her life! Nevertheless, they all pitched in and did everything possible to help, for which I shall be eternally grateful.

However, in spite of our efforts, or perhaps because of them, we found ourselves working mostly at cross-purposes; and with less than a week to go before departure and little if anything accomplished, tempers flared, and we regaled our Spanish hosts with some really beautiful almighty rows. I bet they'd never thought the English could be so good at it! Nevertheless, however baffled they may have been, the Spaniards not only concealed their impressions, but were kindness personified. Don Salvador Moret, for instance, the manager of the hotel, went so far out of his way to help that I cannot find words to express my gratitude. Generally speaking, the whole island brimmed with goodwill in its effort to help the mad Englishman get on with his impossible quest.

Captain Juan Garrido López, a local tug master, is another islander with whom I spent many an enjoyable and instructive hour discussing my problems and exchanging salty tales. He also supplied one of the main problem items on my shopping list, which I had been unable to find anywhere on the island, by very kindly giving me his own personal star finder.

As yet, the actual departure point was still undecided, and I felt the best advice would be that of the local fishermen at San Agustín, about thirty-five miles away. It was agreed that everyone deserved a day off and we would hire a mini-bus and make a holiday excursion of the trip. The day dawned bright and beautiful, and we all piled into the ram-shackle blue minibus and set off along a fine arterial road, which was soon forsaken for a steep, narrow, windy cliff-hanger climbing up the side of an extinct volcano. Our mini-bus creaked, groaned, grunted and almost ground to a halt many times; but luckily, having reached the crater and taken each other's photographs grouped around it, we were soon down the other side and at the promised village.

We found the fishermen sitting on their haunches in a row, propped against the shady side of a wall. Our girls thought they made a very picturesque sight, and indeed they did—a weather-beaten and suntanned group in the shade of that brilliant day. Actually, we were very fortunate to have found them there at all: it was only the wind—wrong for them and, incidentally, wrong for me—that had prevented them from being at sea.

I joined the men—immediately ruining the picture!—and accepted their advice that I leave from San Agustín rather than from Las Palmas, as this would allow me to clear the western tip of Grand Canary Island right away. I chatted with them for a while and then, mission accomplished, climbed back into the minibus with the others for the bumpy ride home.

Back at the hotel, Don Salvador said there was a hotel very near the village of San Agustín, right on the beach, and he would arrange matters so that I could leave from there. This would be ideal.

Around this time a big American ketch bound for the West Indies, the *Camelot*, entered port, and as the Americans, two former test pilots, were in no particular hurry, they offered to give *Britannia* a tow to San Agustín.

By then the Marconi was fully operational, and all that remained to be done was make a few last-minute purchases: transistor radio; rope; fresh fruit and vegetables for the first week at sea; toiletries; petrol to run the generator. The short-wave transistor radio was an essential addition to my navigational equipment. As I intended to rely throughout on celestial navigation, it was of paramount importance, for the accuracy of my sightings, that I know the correct time to the nearest second. For this, although the Rolex GMT-Master which passed for my ship's chronometer was as good as any wristwatch can be, to be on the safe side I intended to keep an eye on it by checking it against the BBC World Service time signals.

Two coils of half-inch nylon rope, each two hundred feet long, were also essential, to stream the drogues, without which I would not be able to hold my own against contrary winds. And speaking of the Devil: since our arrival the weather had been most unsettled, with winds blowing from the west and southwest almost every day. This, according to my fisherman friends and my Pilot Chart, was a freak situation and could not last much longer, the prevailing winds around the year being the northeasterly trades. Jokingly, they said I had brought the bad weather with me and all would be back to normal once I left. Fact was, *unless* it changed I *could* not leave—which, much as I appreciated the Canary hospitality, was not in the least funny.

The departure date had been set for January 19. I simply *had* to leave then, the nineteenth being the last day of our package tour. My mother, Sylvia and John and Margaret Stevens all had to fly back that very day, or they would be marooned for at least a week: with our finances practically exhausted, an economic impossibility. They had come to see me go. How could I disappoint them? The weather forecast was not encouraging, but we could only hope for the best and get on with it. We spent the eighteenth loading *Britannia* at the Royal Nautical Club. We piled up everything alongside *Britannia* and, as the mountain of supplies and equipment grew (it was the first time we had gathered everything together), I could not believe my eyes. As Uffa was fond of saying, everything had to be stowed away "in an orderly, seamanlike manner." How on earth I could ever manage to accomplish such a feat was beyond my comprehension.

Not surprisingly, I didn't. Although we worked like slaves all day, nightfall caught us with only half the cargo loaded. At eleven o'clock, we gave up in despair. Dumping what was left on deck, we covered the lot with a tarpaulin and heaved *Britannia* into the water. I rowed her out into the harbor to join the *Camelot* and fastened a towrope, and off we went. There was no other way if we were to be in San Agustín by morning.

At first it had been my intention to stay on *Britannia*; but at four knots she rode the tow exceedingly well, and I decided it would be better for me to spend the night sleeping in the relative comfort of one of *Camelot*'s bunks. Somebody could always keep an eye on *Britannia*, and it would not do to start a journey such as mine without a proper night's sleep.

Val Schaeffer, skipper of the *Camelot*, apologized for the lack of comfort, but he needn't have bothered. My mother, Sylvia, Martin, Morag, John Stevens, Margaret, Noel Botham and Jeff White were all on board, adapting themselves to a sailor's life with great joy. Admittedly, my mother, thinking of what the next day would bring for me, was not in a very happy mood, and Sylvia and Morag were a bit under the weather, but they tried their best to be brave and, with the help of a few drinks, succeeded.

It was a beautiful warm, starry night—typical, I knew, of many I would soon experience on my own. Only one thing bothered me: the wind, although just slightly more than a gentle breeze, blew from the west. A freak situation. Everybody said so. Been going on for two weeks. Bound to ease off now. Any day. Tomorrow? Would it be tomorrow?

The *Camelot* dropped her anchor on sandy bottom, roughly a cable off the beach of San Agustín, at eight-thirty in the morning. As her dinghy was too small for everybody, we went ashore in *Britannia*. We had breakfast at the hotel, the Costa Canaria, at a table specially laid for us near the swimming pool, together with Señor Garson, manager of the Costa Canaria, and Don Salvador Moret, who had made the trip from Las Palmas to bid me goodbye. The Spanish press was also there in force, and as the news of our arrival spread, we were engulfed by the curiosity of the hotel guests.

By then, to keep souvenir hunters at bay, *Britannia* had been anchored in a fathom of water some twenty yards off the beach, and I must say that I was a bit reluctant to go back to her. After all, to be mobbed as a hero, even on a one-day basis, was rather pleasant, if somewhat disconcerting. Fortunately, the call of duty proved stronger than vanity, and with a deep sigh of resignation, I made my way back to *Britannia*. Martin lent a hand, and with Noel screaming that unless I left at twelve o'clock it would be too late for him to send the story in time to make the following day's edition of the *Sketch*, we slogged away in a feverish attempt to make *Britannia* shipshape. We thought we were progressing nicely when Stevens appeared alongside, almost drowning himself under a five-gallon plastic bag of water. There were four more bags to come, since I intended to carry twenty-five gallons of water as a standby for emergencies. To keep it drinkable as long as possible, we had asked the favor of having it boiled in the kitchen of the Costa Canaria, and then had all but forgotten about it. Now, except on deck, there was no place to stow it. Proper stowage, of course, would have been belowdecks, in a careful balance so as to keep *Britannia* on an even trim. An attempt to achieve that now, with every hatch full to capacity, looked like a nightmare. The idea was preposterous, yet there was no alternative. It had to be done, and that was that.

Somebody was calling from the beach. What now? My

The frame of *Britannia* being constructed at Clare Lallow's boatyard, Cowes. J. F. left, Uffa Fox right. (TOM HANLEY)

N.B. Unless otherwise indicated, photographs are by John Fairfax.

The launching. Uffa Fox in foreground, J. F. giving a "thumbs up" in the rain. (TOM HANLEY)

mother could not stay any longer: she had to rush to the air-port or miss her plane. She could not see me off after all. Leaving Martin to do what he could, I swam ashore, bracing myself for what was to come. Sure enough, the moment I had her in my arms, my mum, who had been extraordinarily brave up till then, burst into tears, and I felt like a rotten fiend. What could I say that would make any difference? Mothers are mothers, and I was her only son! Finally, unable to prolong the agony, she almost ran away, still crying, while Don Salvador, with a protective arm across her shoulders, guided her through the crowd toward her taxi.

A bitter taste in my mouth, fighting to keep my own tears back, I turned around—bumping into Sylvia, who had to leave as well to catch her own plane, an hour later, and . . . she too was sobbing, her eyes streaming like waterfalls. It was too much! Grabbing her, I smacked a rough kiss on her wet lips, then let her go, and as she fell into somebody else's arms, I sprinted for the sea, yelling that I would see her in Florida.

Women! When will they learn to control their emotions?

Back on *Britannia,* desperately longing to be off and on my own once and for all, I plunged myself into the impossible task of sorting the chaos on her deck into something at least resembling seamanlike order. For this I had less than an hour. Not only impossible, but ludicrous.

Now that my mother, Sylvia and the Stevenses were gone, there was no earthly reason for me to leave in such a hurry, other than to keep the gentlemen of the press happy. "Look, Martin," I said, "I am terribly sorry about this, but for me to leave with *Britannia* in the state she's in would be lunacy. It will take the rest of the day to make her seaworthy, and that's that."

He entirely agreed, and luckily, being a sensible journalist, so did Noel Botham. It was a bloody shame really, the weather being absolutely perfect for setting off. Still, if such was the will of the gods, I had no intention of disputing it. As was to be expected, there was a feeling of general disappointment ashore. Personally, considering how hard I had tried, I doubted if anyone could be more disappointed than myself.

Our party spent the rest of the afternoon relaxing on *Camelot* while I stayed on *Britannia*, gently bobbing at the end of a line astern of the ketch. Once more Martin had been willing to help, but with all that gear on board, two were a crowd, and I told him I would rather work alone.

With no wind or clouds to speak of, the heat was murderous, and the backbreaking job of rearranging the stowage in every single hatch gave me the first taste of what it would be like in the days to come. I can't say I looked forward to it. Every now and then I went over the side to cool off and check *Britannia*'s trim—which, try as I might, never seemed to be right. The truth of the matter was that she was overloaded by at least five hundred pounds, and no amount of shifting would change that.

It was not until evening came that I found a suitable compromise, and by then I was so thoroughly fed up I decided to call it a day. After dinner, Jeff and Noel invited me to go ashore with them, but I declined. Apart from being tired, I felt unsociable and despondent in a way that I feared I might attempt to contend with by getting drunk—which, at this stage, I could definitely do without. Instead I retired early, forgetting whatever misgivings I might have had the moment my head touched the bunk.

All the same, I must have had a restless night, because when Martin woke me up shortly after dawn, I felt anything but enthusiasm. So, this was to be *the* day! Having fought so hard for it, I suppose I should have felt elated by a sense of achievement. After all, this was the realization of an ideal, a childhood dream. Strange, but somehow I failed to grasp the excitement of it.

When the time came, I rowed *Britannia* ashore to repeat the motions of the previous morning with a curious sense of detachment, as if only my body were involved. There was the same crowd, but even as I mingled with them, I could scarcely make out the smiling faces, their cheers reaching me with a muted, hollow echo, as if already lost in the distance. On an impulse I suddenly knelt down and wrote in the wet sand of the beach:

JANUARY 20, 1969, 10:30 A.M.

I had barely finished when a wave ever so gently licked the sand past my feet, and I watched the writing disappear, smiling sadly at the futility of my gesture. It was too late to turn back. Already the sea and I were alone with each other.

PART II

The Log

4

There are approximately three thousand six hundred nautical miles between the isle of Gran Canaria and Miami, Florida—which to me meant at least four thousand nautical miles, since I could not hope to follow a straight course in a rowing boat. The position of San Agustín is 27°40′ North Latitude and 15°40′ West Longitude, and that of Miami 26° North, 80° West. With roughly a hundred miles' difference in the latitudes of the two and the prevailing winds being northeasterly trades, I figured that my best bet was to take a westerly course right from the beginning, as I could not prevent myself from being swept south.

Uppermost in my mind was the thought that every mile lost would have to be recovered the hard way. How hard that would be was made clear by the sea that very first day.

We had started with an extremely light southwesterly breeze, and *Britannia* seemed to enjoy herself as she cheerfully plodded on at a two-knot pace. It took us a few hours to round the Maspalomas lighthouse, and by then the sun was burning down fiercely, so we decided to have a little rest. To be on our own at last called for a celebration of sorts. During the last moments of departure some kind soul had dropped a bottle of beer on deck, and after drinking my fill, I let *Britannia* have the dregs.

After that we dozed away the hottest hours of the day, contentedly drifting in a blue void . . . a lazy spell I was to recall with fondness during the weeks to come. Two hours before sunset the wind increased to Force 3–4, still from the southwest. Luckily, by then *Britannia* had already cleared the island, and I decided to take her on a northwesterly course, keeping the waves more or less abeam. It was the best of a bad choice. Grossly overloaded, she was soon shipping water by the bucketful; but the self-draining system worked to perfection, and she did not seem to mind in the least. *Britannia* was as good a boat as I could have hoped to have. But as we began to know each other, I realized that a lot of things would have to be thrashed out between us two before we could work as a team. For all her graceful lines, she was solid, reliable, self-sufficient and unbelievably steady. Unfortunately, she also had an obstinate mind all of her own, a temperament to match that of a prima donna and, apparently, the virginal conceit of a debutante. There was no doubt, for instance, that she considered herself a much better boat than I was a sailor—or at least, a rower.

Our first clash of wills came when I tried to make her run on a southerly course. We started arguing the moment she felt the wind on her bows, and as the wind increased in force, so did our argument. Bending to the oars with all I had, sweating, cursing, changing the position of the dagger board, trailing a warp, pulling on the port oar alone—try as I might, I could not make her change her mind. Eventually, so drained out I could not even spit, I had to surrender. *Britannia* insisted that if she was going to head anywhere, it would be either southeast or northwest. So there we were, going northwest, *Britannia* rolling heavily up and down the choppy backs of five- and six-foot waves. Whether she enjoyed herself more when I caught a crab or when an untimely wave poured a shower of cold misery over me I cannot say. All I know is that she loved being broadside to the weather, and with a ten-inch freeboard this was no joke to me.

However, my main concern, at the time, was to get as far away from land as possible, so during most of the night I went on rowing. All the same, I knew that our progress, if there had been any, was very slow. Our leeway must have been considerable as well, judging by the solitary eye of the Maspalomas lighthouse, gradually blinking its way from the starboard quarter to dead astern and on to the port quarter. I kept reminding *Britannia* how much she would hate to find herself straddling a bed of rocks in the morning, but she paid no heed and remained uncooperative throughout the night.

So it was that I was left to struggle alone, and when eventually dawn appeared, I was in no mood to appreciate its beauty. All I could see was the dark, rugged silhouette of the island of Gran Canaria high upon the horizon, and I guessed we were no more than fifteen miles from piling up on the cliffs.

Amazingly, not a boat, a fish or even a bird was to be seen. Stifling a yawn and scratching my head, I decided it was a most uninspiring spectacle.

How on earth have I got myself into this mess? I wondered. I kicked *Britannia* to see if she had anything to say about it, but there was no response. I felt hungry, damp, sore, thirsty, sleepy—and no Sylvia to look after my needs.

Most silly, this going to sea without a girl. My first resolution of the day, first day and a bare twenty-odd hours after leaving the beach of San Agustín, was that next time, if there was to be a next time, I would make sure to correct the situation by having a soft, plump passenger.

Finding the increasing rumblings of my stomach a serious

interference with any constructive thinking, I sat down to a meal of pork, boiled eggs and raw onions, after which I felt much better. A steaming cup of tea generously laced with brandy, to go with one of my best cigars, put me back on top of the world. Nothing like a full, satisfied tummy to put things in their right perspective.

I knew that the first days were bound to be somewhat chaotic, but this was no excuse for going about things in the slipshod, unseamanlike manner I had permitted myself so far. Already I was aching, tired and fed up. Very well, I thought; chances are I will feel like this for many a day in the months to come, so let's forget it. To cross the Atlantic single-handed in a rowboat: my childhood dream, what? Whether I fulfilled it or not was now entirely up to me. It had been very nice to rub knees and hold hands across a candlelit table whilst prattling away about the dangerous, romantic excitement to be found in adventure, for the benefit of a beautiful, occasional audience. How easy then for one's ego to bask in the warm promise radiating from spellbound eyes, to forget what it was really like out there! Easy to forget that soon candlelight, and soft curves, and tinkling laughter would become faded, pleasant memories—that soon, once more, one would be left to face the cold, alone. The moment of truth and action. The time to find out if one was capable of living up to the image and stories.

"Aye—and that goes for you too, *Britt*. Stop moaning and pull yourself together. From now on there will be no more skimping. Everything has to be organized. Determination and iron discipline. Whatever happens, there will be no escaping from it, no turning back. Do you hear? For us the die is cast; it is all or nothing. Either the beaches of Florida or the bottom of the sea."

Thanks to our hurried departure, and my neglect, *Britannia's* deck was an eyesore, with bits and pieces of equipment haphazardly strewn all over. To prevent any further drifting toward the island, I streamed the drogue, then set about getting everything shipshape.

Three hours' hard work later, everything was properly lashed and tidily stowed away. Not enough, I was sure, to pass the inspection of Uffa's critical eye without a few sour comments on my seamanship; but the only solution I could see to that would be to dump overboard at least a third of my stores. I also discovered that two of my plastic water containers leaked and that I had lost eight gallons of water, leaving me slightly over fifteen gallons and with over four thousand miles to go—not a very cheerful thought. On the other hand, I was supposed to rely throughout on my water distiller. If that didn't work, eight gallons more or less would not make much difference, except perhaps to prolong the agony for a couple of weeks or so.

Unfortunately, there is no substitute for water. The total volume of body water in the average adult male is about forty-five liters—60 percent of his body weight. Fluid loss through dehydration need reach a deficit only of between 11 and 20 percent to cause delirium, deafness, dimming of vision and, eventually, death. Water requirements will differ depending on environmental stress, the level of the man's activity, his body size and whether or not he is in fit condition. Personally, I would probably need something in the region of half a gallon daily; for this I preferred to rely on the proved reliability of my distilling apparatus, rather than lose valuable time and effort experimenting with the painstaking, laborious methods usually suggested for castaways.

Expecting the first days to be tiring did not make them any less so. Luckily, I have never suffered from seasickness, and this time was no exception. The sky had become overcast, the days and nights cold, and the wind finally changed to northeasterly, all of which made rowing much easier. However, first the dangerous proximity of land and then, as we gradually pulled away from it, the no less dangerous one of a shipping lane prevented me from getting any sleep other than a few minutes snatched here and there through sheer exhaustion. As I had no navigation lights, in order to be seen at night I had to depend on a powerful flashlight, which I carried for this purpose. The presence of ships was most unnerving. Having a limited number of batteries, I could not afford to use the torch any more than was absolutely necessary, and to rely on the alertness of the deck watch of merchant ships would have been, if previous experience was anything to go by, wishful thinking. Eventually I settled down to a routine of sorts, rowing almost nonstop throughout the night and sleeping during the day.

On January 25, my fifth day, after an hour of uneventful rowing whilst struggling to keep a more than usually uncooperative *Britannia* on a straight course, I strained a muscle in my back. At first I thought nothing of it, but gradually the pain increased, finally becoming so agonizing that I could not row any longer. The wind being favorable, the best I could do was let *Britannia* drift to her heart's content, and crawling into my cubbyhole under the self-righting chamber, I allowed myself the luxury of eight hours' undisturbed rest.

The next day my back ached so terribly that I could hardly move. To make matters worse, it was very cold, with no sun to speak of, and the wind had changed and was blowing from the southeast, Force 4–5—which was no good, but there was nothing I could do about it. However, I could not afford to just sit and mope, nursing my misery. For a castaway, and for all practical purposes I was one, nothing can be more dangerous. The first rule of survival is to keep morale high at all times, regardless of difficulties. To admit impotence, real or imaginary, is a soul-destroying attitude, the beginning of the end. With what felt like hot iron burning deep into my back, I could not row, but I did. For brief periods of five or maybe ten minutes, I forced myself to grab the oars and row, row—sometimes biting on a piece of wood, at others screaming my head off into the wind, cursing the gods for all I was worth, perhaps reveling in my torment like a damned soul— until the pain became too unbearable for even madness to endure. Whether by this we managed to cover any worthwhile distance is arguable. Also, from a doctor's point of view, adding further strain to an already strained muscle, ligament or whatever was perhaps not quite the proper way to speed its recovery. This may or may not be so, and I did have bitter arguments with myself about the pros and cons of the situation. All I knew was what my training and instinct told me. If at the very beginning of my journey I allowed a momentary physical ailment to take the upper hand, sooner or later I would indulge myself in other weaknesses. How could I hope to emerge the victor in my battle against the sea if I was unable to conquer my own flesh?

Thus, during the first day after my injury, I managed, off and on, to put in two hours at the oars. I went on improving upon this, and by January 29 I was feeling much better— which was just as well, as the weather took a definite turn for the worse.

Jan. 29   *9th day*
Position: 26°17′ North, 17°30′ West.
Bugger all! Most disappointing, as it gives a daily average of only eighteen miles. True, I have not been able to row properly for the last few days and the wind is blowing from the wrong direction, but still hard to take. I must try to do forty miles per day at all costs. Ironic thing to say just now, since the wind is from the southwest, Force 4–5, and I must perforce lie to the drogue to prevent being blown to Africa.
1200 GMT: A plane from the Spanish Coast Guard has paid us a visit.

We did not know it at the time, but *Britannia* and I had been chosen for a practice "Search and Find" exercise. Their company, as they circled over us, was a welcome distraction, further enlivened by some low passes when they buzzed us, engines roaring right overhead. Once they came in so low, wing tips barely skimming the wave tops, that for a moment, watching what appeared to be a head-on collision course with little *Britannia* at the receiving end, I was sorely tempted to jump overboard and go for a swim. In fact, I already had one foot on the gunwale when the pilot suddenly pulled up and away at the very last moment. The son of a gun must have known I am allergic to airplanes! On their last pass, flying at a safer altitude, they dropped a smoke flare, which made me wonder what they were after. Was there a message attached to it? If so, how on earth could they have been so thoughtless as to drop it a full three hundred yards upwind from my position? Surely even a pilot should have had the sense to realize that by the time I had hauled in the drogue the distance would be greater still and that however small she might look from up there, *Britannia* was not a toy boat for a single man to row against a fifteen-knot wind. Yet they repeatedly flew as low as they could over the spot where I could see a bright object of sorts bobbing up and down, trailing a thin column of white smoke. I was convinced there had to be a message attached to it.

What could it be? Obviously it had to be some news of tremendous importance to warrant such a delivery method, but what could have happened? I had been in radio contact with London the day before, and my next call was due in three days. It was hard to believe they could not have waited till then. Annoyed beyond words when I realized that unless I took prompt action, the chances of my ever getting to where the flare was floating were diminishing by the minute, I put in an hour of some of my hardest rowing to date.

Can anyone imagine my wrath when I discovered that I had half-killed myself for the possession of an empty, useless, utterly worthless canister intended for the study of currents and wind drifts? The stupidity of it all left me speechless.

I spent the rest of that day in a mood of sullen disappointment, my disenchantment further enhanced by the end of my fresh food supplies. From then on the mainstay of my diet would be Archie de Jong's dehydrated, high-caloric emergency rations. Here is what I thought of them:

Archie's food is the most horrible thing I have ever had in my life. I just cannot imagine what I am going to think about it a month or more from now. Still no fish.

That was another baffling thing. Since my departure I had not seen a single fish. I could still remember, with a grimace, the wrangling discussions I had had with so-called experts about the survival possibilities, in my opinion unlimited, offered by the sea to the self-reliant castaway.

Here I would like to affirm that I am, and always have been, a great admirer of the French doctor Alain Bombard. Dr. Bombard's theories have been the butt of untold abuse and polemic, notwithstanding the fact that he had the extreme courage and confidence to prove his point in the only possible way.

On October 19, 1952, he set out from the Canary Islands in a flimsy rubber raft, *L'Hérétique*, with no company other than his unshakable, staunch conviction that, to use his own words:

Statistics show that ninety per cent of the survivors of shipwrecks die within three days, yet it takes longer than that to perish from hunger and thirst. When his ship goes down, a man's whole universe goes with it. Because he no longer has a deck under his feet, his courage and reason abandon him. Even if he reaches a lifeboat he is not necessarily safe. He sits, slumped, contemplating his misery and can hardly be said to be alive. Helpless in the night, chilled by the sea and wind, terrified by the solitude, by noise and by silence, he takes less than three days to surrender his life. They are killed not by the sea, not by hunger or thirst, but by their own terror. This need not be so. The survivor of a shipwreck, deprived of everything, must never lose hope. The sea is a natural element, dangerous without doubt, but nevertheless rich enough in the necessities of life to ensure survival until the arrival of aid, or the sighting of land.*

Dr. Bombard sailed *L'Hérétique* from the Canaries to Barbados in sixty-five days. Throughout the entire journey, he depended for food exclusively on fish and seabirds, on fish juice and rain for water and on plankton for Vitamin C. In the process he lost fifty-five pounds in weight, became seriously anemic, lost his toenails, developed serious defects in his vision and suffered dehydration of the skin and a rash covering his whole body, but he got there—alive. Opposed to which his physical condition was irrelevant, as is (to my mind at least) the opinion of those hifalutin experts who, from the cozy smugness of laboratories and conference halls, have since contrived to belittle Bombard's achievement by supposedly sound scientific theories.

The reason for my interest in Dr. Bombard's theories, and my lengthy arguments with the soilbound intelligentsia, had been my own pet theory that slow-moving boats like *Britannia* would attract so many fish, even in the middle of the Atlantic, that with no fishing gear other than a spear gun, I would be able to catch enough not only to survive but, if necessary, to supply myself with all the energy and strength I would need to go on rowing almost indefinitely. This, I was told, was impossible. I would never find enough fish in the middle of the Atlantic, and the few I might find I would certainly not be able to catch with a spear gun alone. It was argued that even though Dr. Bombard had survived, he had barely done so; it had been nothing short of a miracle—and that in any case, he was able to limit his exertions to a minimum. My contention was that if Dr. Bombard had suffered so much, it was mainly from lack of water (which I hoped to

* Bombard, Alain, *The Voyage of the* Hérétique. New York: Simon and Schuster, 1954.

J. F. and Sylvia Cook taking supplies to *Britannia* in Las Palmas,
January 19, 1969. (DAILY SKETCH)

J. F. tries out the cooking arrangements (left) and the water-distillation equipment (below) at Las Palmas. (DAILY SKETCH)

carry on board in the required quantities), and that Dr. Bombard's objective had been simply to stay alive as a castaway might have to, relying entirely on his own resourcefulness, such as making a harpoon with his knife, hooks from fish bones and fishing lines with strands from lanyards. I not only was better equipped, but had implicit trust in my spear gun and ability to use it. All I needed was the fish.

Jan. 30   *10th day*
Wind from the southwest, Force 3.
This is bad. My average since leaving San Agustín has been extremely poor. If the wind doesn't blow from the northeast I will spend a lot of time around here.
1200 zone time: Wind stopped, Force 2–1. Sea calm except for heavy swell, first time since I left. At last it will give me a chance to pull myself together. Incredibly, I have still to see my first fish. The only sign of life is a few small, dark birds, tirelessly fluttering up and down the waves, inches from the water. I have yet to see one catch anything. No ships. Don't think there will be any for a long time, as I am now out of the shipping lanes. If one comes I will try and get their attention and see if I can scrounge a pair of jeans, as my old ones gave up today. Physical condition excellent; hope it stays so.
Temperature at 1600 zone time 23° Centigrade.*
Dusk, hour of dreams, hour of unrealities. It certainly looks so, but this is for real. I feel tired, a little depressed, but otherwise O.K. The depression comes mainly from having come so little after so much effort, but I have promised myself not to be angry at the sea. Nobody asked me to come, and the sea is doing what it always has done; too bad if I don't like it. I intend to win this battle, and the only way of doing it is to arm myself with patience. It will probably take me four months to reach Florida, but . . .
Soon Venus, my favorite goddess, will be out for a shot. Ter-

* 73.4° Fahrenheit.

rible this lack of feminine company. Still no wind. Plan to row all night. Position 27°20′ North, 18° West. This means I have been losing ground. It puts me twenty miles to the southwest of the Isle of Hierro. Because of clouded horizon cannot see any sign of it, but if my fix is correct, should be there. Rowed two hours. Wind suddenly sprang from the west, Force 5; impossible to continue. Hove to.

Jan. 31   *11th day*
Wind from the west, Force 4–5.
Attempted to row, but impossible. Forced to lie to drogue all day. Two drogues. Cloudy and cold. Sighted Hierro in the afternoon; bearings confirm position. Could not do a thing all day except clearing things generally.

Feb. 1   *12th day*
Wind still from the west, Force 4–5.
Heavy swell and spray. Impossible to raise aerial for contact with London. Could not move. Too cloudy to see land. Situation bad. Have exhausted supplies for two weeks without getting anywhere; if the wind does not change, afraid I will not have enough stores to make it to Florida.

Feb. 2   *13th day*
Wind finally dropped some but still from the west, Force 2–3. I am rowing like a slave only to keep more or less the same position, but gradually losing ground. It is just not possible for one man to row against winds Force 3, 4, 5 without losing ground, as one must rest, and it is inevitable to drift back. This cannot go on forever, but it is very trying all the same.

Feb. 3   *14th day*
Wind southwest, Force 4–5.
Another day of the same. Too tired to write.
Rowed 13 hours.

Feb. 4   *15th day*
Wind from the southwest, Force 4–5, gusting 6.
I will finish in Africa at this rate. Have not slept for two days.
Absolutely dead.
Rowed 10 hours.

Feb. 5   *16th day*
Wind from the southwest, Force 4–5.
Is this a joke? Where are the trades? I have had nothing but
southwesterlies and westerlies since leaving San Agustín. I
won't be able to fight against them for very much longer.
Every time I pull the oars now the boat seems to weigh ten
tons. I never thought one could get so tired—but as long as
this wind blows, resting is out of the question.

I cannot remember ever reading a single account of a long
voyage in a sailing boat without coming across a usually bitter complaint by the crew about the unpredictable vagaries
of the wind. However, unless they are in a particular hurry
to arrive somewhere, the tendency is to refer to a lack of
wind, rather than its presence from the wrong quarter, in the
wrong place, at the wrong time of year. Quite understand-
ably, since a becalmed sailing boat is a dead one, whereas a
head wind, if not ideal, can be dealt with by tacking. From a
rower's point of view, there are no such niceties. For him, the
direction of the wind is all-important at all times. Getting
from A to B in a rowing boat can be achieved only in an
absolute calm or with the wind dead, or as dead as can be,
aft. A boat with shallow draft—or, as in the case of *Britannia*, no draft to speak of—can expect very little help from the
currents. The upper layer of the sea, to a depth of several
feet, blows along with the wind, irrespective of the current's
course. By the same token, a small boat lying to a drogue in a
strong wind will not remain stationary. Her drift will be
greatly reduced but not stopped. After all, the purpose of a

drogue (more familiarly, if incorrectly, called a sea anchor) is to keep the head of a ship into the wind in order to meet the waves in the most favorable position. It normally consists of a parachute-shaped canvas which is streamed from the bow on a length of rope and which, once submerged, will open with the pull of the ship and, filled by water pressure, act as a brake. The principle is the same as that of a parachute.

Most yachtsmen never use drogues (a long warp, if properly used, can be as effective, while subjecting the ship to less strain), but to me they were almost as vital as the oars. The pleasures of the lone sailor who, whenever he feels like it (weather permitting), decides to laze away the hours sunbathing or catching up on lost sleep while his boat goes on, effortlessly devouring miles on a preset course, are denied lone oarsmen. A boat without way on her cannot be steered. *Britannia* would be alive only for as long as I manned the oars. The only line that separated her from being a brave, graceful, purposeful little boat and being a brightly colored bit of flotsam was my will to row.

Also, I was beginning to feel some concern about our position. Because of the weather, my last fix was six days old. Since then, I had been able to see the sky only in the pictures of a holiday brochure I had kept as a souvenir. It was my assurance that while everybody in England was living in wet, freezing misery, under permanently clouded skies, I was one of the lucky few to whom "Life in the Canary Isles is continuous basking in sunshine" during the day and offered "incredibly warm, moonlit nights melting with romance." In addition, my weather charts stated that westerly and southwesterly winds were seldom experienced in this part of the world. Telling *Britannia* that somebody had obviously goofed would not improve matters. Besides, I could hardly expect her to believe it was not I, especially after my performance of the previous day.

Desperate for at least a clue on our whereabouts, I had

spent half an hour tinkering with a toy radio direction finder attached to my transistor radio. The result had placed us somewhere in the middle of the Sahara. With *Britannia*'s confidence in me stretched to the limit, my apologetic explanation that electrical and mechanical gadgets were the bane of my life would have done little to ease the tension. It is quite doubtful, anyway, that she would have bothered to listen. After lying to the drogue all day, with no indication from me as to whether I would ever man the oars again, she was clearly on nonspeaking terms with me.

To hell with her! After fifty hours without sleep, nearly half of which I had spent at the oars, I was exhausted. What was the use of rowing when to make progress against a fifteen-to-twenty-mile-per-hour wind was impossible? Why burn all my energies for nothing? In any case, I was the captain and it was my prerogative to decide what to do. I had decided that as long as the wind stayed to the southwest we would lie to a drogue, and that was that! This did not mean I could rest in peace—as *Britannia* retaliated by refusing absolutely to remain head-on to the waves. The drogue abetted her by becoming fouled at least once every hour.

I had four drogues, all exactly the same: a) too small to hold a boat like *Britannia*; b) too light and flimsy to withstand the pressure without breaking and c) encumbered by the fact that I had no swivel. In my four years at sea, spent mostly on rather big and fast power craft, I had never seen, let alone used, a drogue. Because of my ignorance on the subject, I had relied entirely on advice. Nobody had seen fit to suggest that a drogue attached to a warp without a swivel would become a tangled mess in no time at all. Uffa Fox had never mentioned it, in spite of his lengthy explanations of the many ways a drogue can best be put to use, because, he being Uffa, it had probably never occurred to him that anyone could be so appallingly stupid as to need to be told the obvious. As for the others—to suggest that they had never used one would be rude and uncalled-for, so I will assume that they too considered it unnecessary to explain the self-evident. The fact is, I did not have a swivel, did not have the means of making one and, therefore, could never rely on the drogue to do its job without constant attention.

A dense, filthy-gray mantle of scud, permanently hovering over the horizon, reduced my visibility to a couple of miles. Even with the drogue working properly, our rate of drift was at least a knot. If I went to sleep in my state of near collapse, my alarm clock could well shrill itself to pieces before I would wink an eyelid. After five days of aimless rowing in one direction and drifting in another, we could be anywhere. I could not row, dared not seek cover from the biting wind in my cubbyhole, dreaded falling asleep and had nothing to do. During the whole day this had been the wretched state of affairs.

It was roughly an hour before I saw it: the first manifestation of life the sea had offered me so far. Slumped on deck, facing the wind and the occasional shower of spray (the better to stay awake), I was keeping a weary eye on the white patch that was my drogue, billowing under the waves at the end of a hundred-foot warp. Something had suddenly bobbed to the surface right on top of it. Getting up to have a clearer view, I lost it from sight. I was beginning to think I had made a mistake when it reappeared, barely a yard or so from *Britannia*—a sea turtle!

Seemingly baffled out of its wits by our presence, it just floated there, so near that I was sure I could grab it if only I leaned over the side. Already it had noticed me, twisting its short neck and blinking a nervous eye in my direction. In my excitement, I had forgotten the hard-learned lessons of my hunting days. Animals are attracted by movement, not shape. Had I kept still, the turtle would have been unable to differentiate between *Britannia* and myself.

Keep still and don't look at it. Steady, or it will dive any moment now. My supper! For Christ's sake, where is that spear gun?

All these days, without even a sardine in sight to shoot at, I had kept the darned thing to hand and ready at all times, and now . . .

"Please don't go away yet, Little One. Hang on, you beautiful, precious thing, you—I promise I won't be a sec. Stay around, please!" Where is that spear gun?

Where it had to be. Lashed along my spare oars on the port side, so tightly anyone would have thought I had been fearing a capsize. Several minutes of frantic fumbling with wet ropes and I was ready to shoot—only there was nothing to shoot at. My precious turtle had gone.

Then I saw it, back at the drogue, where I had first spotted it.

"Can't make out what it is, can you? Why don't you come back here? I will tell you all about it. Come on, Baby, don't be shy. Leave that blasted drogue alone. Come and see the beautiful boat. That's the idea. You like the pretty boat, don't you? You are too far still; come nearer and I will show you something. That's it. Nearer, right alongside, that's my girl. Now keep your head up, stay still. Don't move—there!"

What a shot! From a range of three yards the neck presented a difficult target; but for once *Britannia* cooperated by keeping still at the crucial moment. Although the shot was perfect, however, only the point of the spear had gone through the thick skin, probably hitting bone before the barbs could penetrate. It was a big turtle, a hundred pounds or so, and I feared a strong pull might turn it loose. For the moment, surprise and an inch of cold steel had shocked it into paralysis, but one never knows. Turtles are extremely hardy animals to kill. I had heard of a turtle head's biting a careless foot half an hour after being severed from the body.

Hoisting my first prey on board was quite a struggle, as it exploded back to life the moment my hands grabbed it. It was amazingly strong and, catching me off balance, nearly had me over the side. I was pulling it on board by the hind legs. It was already halfway in when the forelegs got hold of the gunwale and the turtle suddenly lunged forward—at the very moment chosen by a wave to come tumbling in, the crest breaking on us in blind fury. The sea defending its own! *Britannia* gave a mighty lurch and I fell, my knees hitting the deck with a thump of searing pain, my thighs wedged against the side while my body stretched overboard as far as it would go, shoulders, head and arms underwater, still holding the turtle.

"You bitch! I will follow you to the bottom of the sea before I let go."

The ensuing tug-of-war ought to have been the delight of the gods. As for Venus, how she must have laughed! But I won in the end; and that night, and for days afterward, I ate my fill of turtle stew. I have never tasted a better one, before or since. My very own recipe, too, created on the spur of the moment. Regrettably, I have forgotten the ingredients; it must have been one of those once-in-a-lifetime strokes of culinary genius.

Feb. 6   *17th day*
Wind from the west, Force 2–3.
Not so bad, at last. Still from the wrong way, but at least can try to go south a bit. Will do so as soon as I get through to London.

According to the schedule worked out in England between Independent Television News and the *Daily Sketch*, I was supposed to attempt contact with them, through Baldock Marine Radio Station (GBC 4), every four days at 0800 GMT. Failing that, every day afterward until, hopefully, we would establish contact.

With a range of five thousand nautical miles, my compact Marconi radio (as long as its watertight compartment remained watertight) should, in theory, be up to the task at all stages of the journey, provided—and there, I soon discovered, lay the crux of the matter—I was able to raise the aerial to a height of twenty-odd feet. To do this I had to attach the aerial to a hydraulic mast, clamp it against the forward self-righting chamber, pump it up to the required height and there you were. Or there it was—during the trials in the calm, secluded waters of Las Palmas harbor. Out here it was an entirely different cup of tea. *Britannia* simply hated the sight of a metallic rod gracelessly sticking out of her skin, and if there happened to be any sea about, she would go positively mad. Pitching, rolling, shaking, she behaved with such excited frenzy that in a matter of minutes, she contrived to wrench the wildly whipping aerial from its bracket.

As the radio cubicle was aft, I had to make my calls crouching between the generator on one side and the gas stove and gimbals on the other, continually scrambling in and out every time the aerial snapped away.

For all my efforts, I had been able to get through only twice so far, and I was beginning to regard the whole business with distaste. If I could get through today, I wouldn't have to think about it for four days. Otherwise, I would have to try again tomorrow. Damn it! Why couldn't they hear me?

"Hello, GBC 4, hello GBC 4, this is *Britannia*, *Britannia*, Atlantic rowboat *Britannia* calling GBC 4, calling GBC 4. Come in GBC 4, come in GBC 4. *Britannia* calling GBC 4, come in please, come in please."

At last they heard me. "Hello, *Britannia*, hello *Britannia*. GBC 4 to *Britannia*. Reading you loud and clear. How do you read me? Over."

Naturally, the first thing they wanted to know was my position and how things were going. What could one say to that? How does one say that after seventeen days at sea, one is probably still within spitting distance of the point of departure?

5

Feb. 7   18th day
Wind from the northwest, Force 2–3.
Rowing south, but too tired to take full advantage of this
change of wind. Come what may, tonight I intend to sleep at
least eight hours at a stretch. There is a limit to what one can
do, and I think I have reached mine.

Feb. 8   19th day
Slept as planned. Wind changed during the night to west,
Force 4–5, and drogue, naturally, fouled up. The gods know
how much we have drifted! Hard to believe, but looks as if it
will be a sunny day. Sighted a ship 0930 GMT. Stopped three
to four miles from us, downwind.

"Hey, *Britt*, what do you make of it? Think they have seen
us? If so, seems daft to stop so far away. Maybe they have

engine trouble. Think we ought to go over and have a look-see? Maybe we can get some grub. Decent grub. I'm fed up with turtle. A shower too. Come on. We may never get another chance. Let's row!"

It took me the best part of an hour to pull alongside, and I still had not been able to make up my mind about what I was going to request for breakfast. By then the crew were lining the decks, cheering, and urging us to round the stern to the lee side.

"They probably think we are shipwrecked, *Britt*. We will give them the surprise of their lives!"

"What ship are you from?" somebody yelled, and I laughed.

"Ship? This one! Her Majesty's Rowboat *Britannia*. Why? Need a tow?"

It was their turn to exult, and the roar of their laughter still fills me with happiness. The *Skauborg*, a Norwegian ship, had sprung an oil leak and they had had to stop to repair it. While this was being done she would remain hove to, and I was invited on board.

Already they had a rope ladder over the side, and after securing *Britannia*, I scrambled up, stepped on deck and, but for a pair of strong, helpful arms, would have fallen on my face. After *Britannia*'s, the *Skauborg*'s deck was rock-steady, and my legs were at a loss as to how to walk around on a platform that refused to move with them.

The first thing I was offered was a shower. Then, scrambled eggs; bacon; cold, frothy beer; strong coffee; cigars— heavenly bliss is the only way to describe it.

The master of the *Skauborg*, Captain Block, as indeed did everybody else, went out of his way to make me feel at home. The radio officer, a former journalist, insisted on taking all sorts of pictures and a detailed account of my experiences and feelings so far, just in case—he was sure I would understand—they were the last people to see me alive. One never knew; after all, I was risking my neck, wasn't I? And if the worst happened, it would be terrible if the world's papers were deprived of a picture to go with the story. In these cases one must be practical; surely I understood?

Not to be outdone, I took some pictures myself. After all, as he put it, one has to be practical, and big ships also have been known to founder.

What a lovely day! As repairs in the engine room seemed to be taking longer than expected, the Captain invited me to stay for lunch, and how could I refuse? If my experiences at sea entitle me to a modest word of counsel, I would like to suggest to all future shipwrecked mariners that they try their very best, whenever possible, to be rescued by a Norwegian ship. It was a castaway's dream.

Unfortunately, my position could hardly have been worse. We were in the middle of a shipping lane, eighty-three miles southwest of the isle of Gran Canaria. Eighty-three miles after nineteen days at sea—and all that rowing! Why, I had been twenty miles farther four days after leaving San Agustín! Now, all because of those blasted winds, the entry in my Log reads:

. . . to be only eighty miles away after nineteen days at sea and so much rowing makes my heart cry. What the hell, it is really too much! Captain Block said he had never known southwesterly winds at this latitude before. He gave me American Pilot Charts which show such winds to be almost nonexistent in this area at this time of year. Why did it have to happen to me? Somebody up there obviously doesn't like us. Oh, well . . .

The Captain suggested that, considering the circumstances, if I decided to give up my crazy attempt, he would be all too pleased to give me a free passage. He was bound for Buenos Aires. Buenos Aires, where my mother, home and most of my friends were! To realize the full extent of my temptation, one ought to consider that no one before had attempted to row across the Atlantic single-handed, and no one at all had ever rowed from east to west. In the light of my experiences so far, how could I know if it was at all possible?

Britannia had never looked so puny and forlorn to me as when we were back on our own, with only the sea and sky to look on us. Blasting her siren in salute, the *Skauborg* had pulled away; gathered speed; become small, smaller, a black speck on the horizon—gone. The wind laughed, but I was not ashamed and did not try to hide my tears.

Feb. 9   *20th day*
Wind from the northwest, but mainly west, Force 3–4.
Heading south but drifting toward east. Progress very slow.
Rowed ten hours.

Feb. 10   *21st day*
Wind from the west, Force 2–3.
Fighting on. Position at noon 26°23′ North, 16°00′ West.
Ship stopped to ask if I needed anything; said no, except a cold beer. Gave me one. Ship, Bobody, bound for Rio. Second ship, Greek, Enotis, passed by two hours later. Did not stop, as I signaled did not need anything. Am O.K. physically, but morale very low. All this rowing to make an average of five miles per day, and even this south instead of west, is very depressing. However, the wind must eventually change. I will try to go as far south as 20° North Latitude and then hope for better luck. At this rate it will take me a hell of a long time to get there—but by the gods, I will do it!
Rowed ten hours.

Feb. 11   *22nd day*
Wind from the northwest. Makes for awkward rowing and is pushing us toward the African coast. Very bad day. All the time at night we are afraid of being run down by some ship.

This is like Piccadilly Circus. In daytime they pass by, if they are near enough to spot us (and this means two to three miles), wave and go on. Good luck to them; I hope we will get some ourselves one day.

Feb. 12   *23rd day*
Can't believe it! Wind from the northeast, Force 4.
I just threw away a mirror I had broken the day of my back injury, finally deciding it was a bad thing to have on board. One hour afterward, the wind came from the northeast. Am I getting superstitious in my old age? God damn it all, let's row! Very good rowing all day. I am now much happier; I only hope it lasts. Greek ship, Argonaftis, stopped by at 1800 GMT. Gave position 25°29' North, 16°11' West. Also some cabbages, lettuce, canned vegetables and a loaf of bread. Rowed twelve hours.

Feb. 13   *24th day*
Wind still from the northeast.
This is good. All the same, I have lost a month, and I am beginning to think I will never make it to Florida before the end of May, perhaps even later. This I don't like at all, as the hurricane season begins in June, but there is nothing I can do about it. Rowing alone is a tremendous handicap, as one must rest and there is a limit to the hours one can row; in fact, I have barely time to do anything except rest and row. Ten hours as an average may not sound much out of twenty-four, but they are killing. Britannia is a very good boat, but she just won't run with the wind aft and all the time is trying to get broadside to the waves.

This unwillingness of *Britannia*'s to run on a straight course with the wind aft was her most infuriating fault. Perhaps I should say her only one; but it was a serious defect, and an energy- and time-consuming one. Ideally she ought to have behaved like a surfboat, but she never did. This was probably due to a slight imbalance caused by excessive windage on the fore and aft self-righting chambers.

In the original Uffa Fox design, they were supposed to be the same as on his airborne lifeboats: made of rubber, and inflatable or deflatable at will. Unfortunately, technical and financial difficulties had prevented the adoption of similar rubber chambers for *Britannia* in the short time available. Eventually, it had been decided to have them built from Plastazote, an expanded polythene, kindly donated by the manufacturer, Expanded Rubber and Plastics, Limited. Whilst extremely light and almost indestructible by climatic wear and tear, and with a buoyancy of thirty pounds per cubic foot, it proved to be an ideal solution—except that the chambers, or blisters, thus were rigid, permanent structures. Undeniably, they provided a great advantage over the original rubber ones in all respects but one: windage. In the engine-powered airborne lifeboats this would probably have made little difference. To me it was hell. I had foreseen this, of course, but had decided that in the long run, the disadvantages would be balanced by the advantages. I still think the same. After all, extra windage works both ways—or should have, if only the rudder surface had been greater. In my opinion, *Britannia* would not surf simply because the moment she started to ride a wave crest, her natural tendency to yaw was immediately increased by the pushing of the wind on the self-righting chambers; and at our speed, once a yaw had begun, the rudder surface was simply not great enough to counteract it. The only way was for me to pull on one oar almost twice as hard as on the other, unnecessarily spending my energy and continually interrupting the regular rhythm of my stroke. Also, I had to be very quick on the ball. Unless I applied correction at the very onset of the yaw, it would be too late: I would lose control, *Britannia* would broach and, if the next wave happened to be a rotter—most were—we were in for a cold shower. This was particularly irritating as it usually happened after I had managed to dry out from the previous dousing and was beginning to feel warm again. The general effect on my nerves was as repetitive as it is unprintable.

Feb. 15   *26th day*
Wind from the east, Force 2–3—weak but very helpful.
I am now at 25° North Latitude, the same as Florida. If I could only row due west from now on without drifting south too much!
At 1600 GMT a giant tanker passed, the Bulford. *So big, in fact, that when they asked me if I needed assistance, I couldn't resist the temptation of stopping them for food— which I really needed anyway, being so far behind schedule. They gave me enough canned food for two weeks and four loaves of bread. Went aboard for fifteen minutes to have a shower. Gave my position as 25°05′ North, 16°45′ West (my own reckoning was only five miles off—not bad considering I had taken my last sight forty hours before. This makes me very happy, as it means that after five years without practice, I have worn off the rust and my former navigational skill has come back with a bang). They promised to inform ITN and the* Daily Sketch *everything is as fine as can be. I spoke to them this morning, but reception was appallingly bad and I am not sure whether or not they received me. I certainly did not receive them and was very sorry about it, as I spoke with Sylvia and could hardly understand a word she said. I am missing her very much—and this is indeed very strange, as I never think of my girls when on a caper. Must be getting old. All the same, she is a wonderful girl, and I am glad I am smart enough this time to appreciate it.*
Rowed ten hours.

Feb. 16   *27th day*
Wind from the east, Force 1–2, later veering to southeast, Force 3–4. Feel all right but very tired. Still, if the wind

J. F. demonstrates his method of spearfishing for food, prior to the departure. (DAILY SKETCH)

A view of the generator, taken after departure.

holds, tomorrow I hope to reach 18° West Longitude—which is where I was January 29, before being blown back. All these days, nearly a month now, and I am still making no progress —just trying to get back to where I was nine days after leaving San Agustín! True, I am one hundred and twenty miles south of that position; but I am aiming west, not south, and this is very depressing.

Strange as it may seem, I have seen practically no fish yet since I left, except for the turtle and a couple of sharks. I could really do with some fish meat to change my diet. It is now sunset, and as I have been rowing most of the day, I feel tired and, for the first time, in a contemplative mood. Guess I am beginning to feel the loneliness. All the same, it is a magnificent sunset; the sea is like a mirror; no wind at all; nearly no clouds except a few in the west—and I wonder, also for the first time, What the hell am I doing here? Money? No, people don't do this sort of thing for money, certainly not me. There are far easier ways. Glory, then? Perhaps a bit of that. Or am I trying to prove something? To myself or others? Surely not to others. And to myself? What can I prove to myself that I don't know already? What, then? Maybe I will find the answer before the journey is finished. And maybe I won't. What does it matter? I am enjoying myself, doing something I have yearned to do for sixteen years, and there is not a single thing I regret, whatever the outcome. I am doing what I have always loved to do, being part of and fighting against Nature. Perhaps that is what it is. I know She doesn't care, but look at the beauty of it all! Vast, cruel, indifferent to whether I am here or not, or anybody else for that matter, but who cares? I have accepted Her challenge, and in trying to beat Her in such a primitive way I am not doing more than thousands, millions of men have done before me, and will go on doing. Fighting Nature at Her rawest! Could there be a more beautiful thing? Whether I lose or win is beside the point. What matters is the struggle—uneven, yes, but well worth fighting for. Insignificant, little as I feel at the moment,

I cannot but feel proud of myself, and if I end at the bottom
of the sea, it won't make any difference. I shall give as much
as I can take. The sea can certainly break, destroy me, if such
is his whim, but bend my will, conquer me? Never! And if
these are bold words, let them be so. I love you, Sea, and if I
soon will be cursing you again, at least tonight we are at
peace with each other. Let us enjoy it, and hell take tomor-
row. After all, whether you care, or like it, or not, you are part
of me, and I might soon become part of you.
Rowed ten hours.

Bold words indeed. And as time passed, and the weeks
stretched into months, many were the occasions I had to
question their wisdom. Still, I never really regretted them.
They had come from the heart, not the brain, and when the
odds against the success of my venture seemed to become all
but overwhelming; when gale after gale, illness, hunger, in-
juries, exhaustion to and beyond the limits of human endurance joined forces and drove me out of my mind, obliterating
from it any sense of purpose—in fact, the very reason for my
existence—it was the heart that refused to surrender, to see
the utter madness, hopelessness of it all, and by keeping alive
the beast within me, allowed me to recover and become a
man once more. Could there be a better victory or reward for
the human spirit? Is there any need to be reasonable, logical,
coherent even, about what makes men, each in his own way,
reach for the stars?

Feb. 17   *28th day*
So you heard me, bloody bastard! Didn't lose any time, either.
What do you expect to achieve by this? Make me lose more
time, that's all. Damn everything to hell and back! Winds
from the southwest, Force 4–5, at night increasing to 6–7;
waves fifteen feet high—a gale, in other words. There is noth-
ing I can do except lie to a drogue. Had it been from the

northeast or east, I would have tried to run before it, but as it is I can only curse. Very bad night, as drogue kept fouling up and had to watch it and work like mad all night. Thoroughly wet, cold, angry beyond words. To make it worse, in the early morning, when it wasn't so bad yet, a beautiful fish came round. I speared it, the knot attaching the line to the spear came loose and it went away, taking the spear with it. I want a fish badly, to change my diet.

Rowed three hours only, after which I had to pack up. I not only wasn't making any progress but was losing ground faster than I would with the drogue.

Feb. 18   29th day
Wind from the southwest, Force 6–7, all day and night. No comment except—damn it all!

A gale at sea in a small boat is something I understood and, up to a point, enjoyed. I have always thought it is during a gale, rather than a hurricane, that the awesome power the sea is capable of unleashing is best appreciated. Some things are better imagined than lived. My anger was not so much at the sea as at the wind. Southwest was the very worst quarter from which it could come—as rotten and foul a blow as could be. Hate—brutal, single-minded, animal hate, born of impotence and frustration—was my only defense against it. The thundering charge of the sea, the plunging cascades of white fury one could fight, hit, taste, spit at. It was there! But the wind—the wind was everywhere, nowhere; could not be seen, only heard, laughing, always laughing, the God-damned laugh of the wind; pressing, pushing, destroying in an hour the slavery of days.

Britannia, a brightly colored little toy, hides in the troughs, reels on the crests, wallows in the slopes, gathers momentum; a vicious jerk from the drogue checks her, then releases her, and she staggers, crabwise, dazed.

"Pull yourself together, *Britt*—don't just stare. Head-on to it!"

Too late. A breaking wave has just seen the opening, rears, whirls and hisses in gleeful anticipation. Smothered in foam, *Britannia* cringes back, shudders—then plunges forward, her brave, battered little soul undaunted, ready to fight again.

Yes, the sea could destroy us; but for that he would need all his might, all his might. "We will never give up. Never! Do you hear? Never!" Whacked, swamped, knocked about, we struggled on, with me screaming defiance into the night. There was little else we could do.

Feb. 19   *30th day*
Wind from the southwest, Force 4–5.
Could not raise aerial. Waves still very high in spite of wind reduction. Impossible to row and, since the last three days have been overcast, I have no idea of our position. Today it had been my intention to reach 19° West Longitude, and now we are probably back to 16°. Are we ever going to get out of this trap? The gravity of this problem is increasing by the day. Unless we can get out of here within the next week or two, we will never beat the hurricane season to Florida. We had a month to spare when we left; now we have none and are really pressed by time. Since leaving we have had eighty-five percent southwesterly winds—this in an area where there is supposed to be almost nothing else but northeast-erlies; so much for our luck! Have the gods abandoned me? Where are you, Venus? You, the most brilliant, beautiful body in the sky, have you forgotten me? I haven't made any sacrifices to you for a month now, but what do you expect? I am in the middle of the Atlantic, on my own, in case you haven't noticed; what can I do? Just give me a hand and I promise you the most beautiful orgy I can think of at the other side. You are my star; you have never failed me yet. Why now? Come on, old girl, give me a hand and I will beat the sea. All I need is a break to get out of here, that's all.

Feb. 20   *31st day*
A month to the day, and wind from the southwest, Force 4–5!
I shudder to think how far back we must have drifted. All these days of rowing like mad, all this wasted effort!

Soaked to the bones, tired out of my wits, I had sought satisfaction for my murderous mood through the two unfortunate dorados I had speared early in the day. This fish is more usually called a dolphin—not to be confused with the friendly mammal of the same name—and is a very common species which I had expected to see long before this; but better late than never. Renowned for their unusual speed, dorados live on the surface, chasing and feeding mainly on flying fish. The magnificent coloring of their tapering bodies varies from royal blue to emerald green as they flash through the waves after their prey. They are remarkably beautiful, with yellow tails and a long blue dorsal fin, and can grow to a maximum of six feet in length, weighing sixty pounds.

My two victims had been excessively careless in their curiosity toward *Britannia*. The lumbering pace of her barnacle-studded underbelly undoubtedly inspired confidence. They were not to know until too late of the mortal sting lurking above: too late to pass on the dearly acquired knowledge.

After hanging the last strip of cut-up meat to dry in the wind, I sat back with a sigh. The pitiful bloody remains of the carved-up carcasses were all that was left of the dorados' beautifully tapered grace—stark reminders of how swift the transition from life to death could be out here. No, not only here; it was the same everywhere—always has been and always will be. Life being the cheapest, most expendable commodity of all, kill-or-be-killed is a universal game. Simplicity itself, the rules are easy to learn, easy to teach and easy to abide by.

Finding the sorry mess at my feet increasingly irritating, I got up again and wearily tossed the dorado spoils overboard.

They sank right away, and for a while my eyes were held in morbid fascination by the opalescent zigzags slowly descending to the bottom. I turned in and slept—a restless, harrowed, uncomfortable sleep.

BBBRRRRrrrrrrrrrrrrr . . .

"For Christ's sake stop it! Stop it!"

This time the brain-shattering, loathsome shrill of the alarm clock going off inches away from my head was more than I could stand. In a fit of childish temper, I grabbed the hideous contraption and flung it over the side.

"There! Blast yourself!"

After that, I just leaned back and laughed. I felt so good, but so good, I could have laughed forever.

A cursory glance at my surroundings showed that three hours' sleep had brought little or no improvement in the weather. The sky had remained overcast, the sea choppy, the wind from the southwest. At least my despondency had followed the alarm clock, and dismissing the lot with a shrug, I set about preparing my afternoon tea.

I found the craving for a strong cup of tea overwhelming after waking up, as I always had a dry, salty, bitter tang in my mouth then. With it, instead of the usual cigarette, I resolved to have a pipe. A full one, too! Yes, that would be nice. It would give me time to think how I was going to cook the dorados. How about a sip of brandy as well, to help sharpen the imagination? I was beginning to feel my old self again.

Retrieving the steaming kettle from the stove under the aft blister, I crawled back, once more congratulating myself on the neat arrangement of my cooking department. This consisted of a gimbaled frame clamped on deck at the far end of the chamber. Nicely tucked away out of the weather, the stove was fueled by propane gas, which Calor Gas, Limited, had supplied in one hundred and eighty small disposable containers. Each canister would last from two to two and a half hours, and all I had to do to have the burner going was turn a knob and apply a match to it. No messing about with paraffin and alcohol. The procedure couldn't have been easier at home.

Standing on deck, with the kettle in one hand and my tea mug in the other, I rejoiced in the fine sense of balance my legs had acquired, vowing that come what might, today had seen the last of my fits of temper. Why should I allow anything to spoil my mood?

A sudden, mighty bump shook *Britannia* and sent me sprawling on deck, yelling blue murder as most of the tea, still scorching hot, splashed over my bare legs. Still in a daze, I peered over the gunwale, looking for the cause of the commotion. I was not left in doubt for long. A huge, mean-looking shark swam by, only inches away from my face, staring at me with a cold, unblinking little eye as if daring me to do something about it. Before I could gather my wits, he went under and gave *Britannia* an even stronger thump. My nose seemed to go down as the gunwale came up; they met with a bang, and there I lay, swearing like a trooper, an uncontrollable flood of tears, mixed with blood, streaming down my nose while waves of scalding pain throbbed along my legs.

The indignity of it, by all that is holy, was the last straw. After that I simply *had* to get him.

Easier determined than done. First, as the brutish fellow's single-minded purpose appeared to be the demolition of poor *Britannia*'s bottom, I had to unship the rudder. My steering problems were big enough as it was, and while it is always possible to rig a jury rudder with an oar blade, I would much rather have the use of the conventional one. After that, I fed the shark a few scraps of dorado. I wanted to make sure he didn't go away before I came up with a suitable idea to end his days. Regrettably, this was an occasion when I could not rely on my trusty spear gun. He was too big—about seven to eight feet long, two hundred pounds or over. His general color and appearance were those of a dusky shark, but I was not sure about it.

I could probably have fashioned a harpoon of sorts by lashing my knife to the end of an oar; but I had only one knife and was not keen on the possibility of losing it. Finally I had a brainstorm. Making a loop with the half-inch-thick nylon rope I kept as a spare for the drogue, I soon had a perfectly good, strong lasso, weighed at the sides with some lead wire and a few bolts to make it sink. The free end of it I fastened round a cleat forward. Then, attaching a few yards of string to a big chunk of fish meat, I threw it into the water. Immediately, the shark swam after the bait.

"How about it, *Britt*? The beggar thinks it's dinner time!"

I waited till the shark had the tasty bit right under his nose and then, at the last fraction of a second, as he opened his mouth, gave the string a gentle pull and let him swallow a mouthful of water instead.

Who ever said that sharks are incapable of showing emotion? Mine made his disappointment so obvious it was pathetic. The tantalizing game kept me amused for nearly fifteen minutes—by the end of which the shark had begun to show signs of nervous breakdown.

"I think our friend is ripe for the final laugh, *Britt*. Brace yourself!"

Getting the lasso ready, opened and half submerged in the water, I tempted Dusky for the last time. With my hand pulling the string from inside the loop, it was child's play, as he came rushing after the bait, to guide him right alongside *Britannia* and into the noose. I passed it round the snout and past the gills and, before it could slip over the dorsal fin, tightened with a pull, and there we were—Dusky, the mighty killer, hanging helplessly under the Union Jack.

For a fellow of such dense brain matter, Dusky took a remarkably short time to realize he had been had. When he did, he went berserk, and for a couple of minutes, *Britannia* went for her fastest ride ever—skimming the waves like a torpedo, with me hanging on for dear life. It was hard to believe that even a shark could generate such tremendous power.

However, it did not last for long. Mighty brute he might have been; but as killers go, man is still the best Nature has ever produced, and I was soon able to haul him back alongside, as near drowned as made no difference.*

Before he had time to recover, I shortened the rope till he was halfway out of the water. Then, after passing another coil round his tail, I stretched him along the gunwale and made it fast on the aft cleat. The fight completely gone from him, Dusky took on the appearance of a fresh salami strung out to dry.

Curious about the possible contents of his stomach, I slit him open—and, surprise, surprise, it was not a he, but a she, with about two dozen little sharks in her belly. They were alive, apparently in perfectly good health and, size apart, exact replicas of Mama. Except for a few that managed to wriggle away, I soon had the lot gasping in one of my plastic buckets. The prospects of my immediate future being rather precarious at the time, there was no love lost between us, and my last entry in the Log for that day was:

. . . killed them all and dedicated my victory to Venus. I suppose that is what she wanted; women are all the same. Well, it's now sunset, the wind has almost stopped and, yes, my beautiful star, thank you, I shall row all night.

---

* Sharks obtain their oxygen from the flow of water over their gills. Since the gills do not move independently, they must achieve this by swimming. Thus, it a shark is prevented from moving freely in the water it will, eventually, die from asphyxia—*i.e.*, drown.

6

*A day of absolute calm. Very hot. 35° Centigrade.**

The day before, our position at sunset had been 25°21′
North, 16°35′ West. Forty-odd miles to the east of that and
we would enter the fifty-fathom line of the African coast. A
few more miles farther east and, if not home, we would certainly be dry.

Since then I had rowed ten hours, and at dawn the sky had
been clear, but I had been too tired to bother taking sights.
How far we had come I did not know and did not care, although I knew we couldn't be far from the last fix—which
meant that any westerly wind would land us in Africa. There
was not a thing we could do about it except go on fighting till
we ran out of sea.

At first the day had seemed absolutely ideal for making up

* 95° Fahrenheit.

lost ground, but unfortunately, the sun thought otherwise. In his first windless outing in ages, he soon made his presence overbearing. By midmorning the sea, with not a ripple on it, had the appearance of a dead lake, and I felt as if I were cooking in my own steam. To go on would have robbed me of what little energy I had left, and if the calm persisted into the night, I would lose the best rowing hours through sheer exhaustion. In any case, I badly needed a few hours' sleep, and the opportunity to have them in relative peace seemed too good to pass by. There appeared to be a very slight westerly current—in which I allowed *Britannia* to bask, untrammeled by the drogue. Taking out my spare alarm clock, I set it for three in the afternoon, which would give me, I hoped, five hours' uninterrupted sleep. To make sure this clock didn't follow its predecessor, I put it into a polythene bag and lashed it to a bitt, well out of range.

Waking to find the afternoon heat even more oppressive than that of the morning, I decided to shave. A rather painful operation, being the first since departure, but the luxurious feeling of all-but-forgotten cleanliness proved well worth the effort. After that it was only natural to take things a step further, and getting out the brush and salt-water soap, I gave myself a thorough scrub, followed by a rinse in the sea—during which I decreed the time had come to scrape *Britannia*'s hull free of barnacles, since this would greatly improve our speed.

I could hardly have chosen a better day for this. With flippers, mask and snorkel, I dived into the pleasantly warm water and with my knife began to scrape away the hundreds of barnacles that had managed to attach themselves to the bottom of *Britannia*. They were mostly cirripeds,* and their phenomenal rate of growth astounded me. From the very outset of our journey I had watched these minute organisms, slightly bigger than a pinhead, attach themselves and prolif-

* Marine animals living in valved shells attached to their bodies and whose legs resemble a curl of hair.

erate until now, a month later, the submerged part of *Britannia's* hull was almost completely covered by a forest of inch-and-a-half-long creatures, apparently thriving on a diet of antifouling paint.

They offered little resistance to the knife. Zestfully scraping away, I was soon surrounded by a slowly sinking cloud of cirripeds. I watched them go down like so many fluttering snowflakes, glittering along shafts of light and slowly, ever so slowly, disappearing into the blue gloom below. Floating in an apparently unfathomable void gave me the perturbing feeling that cold, eerie fingers were tingling along my spine. The sort of persistent queasiness one tries to ignore, yet which is there. The impalpable presence of the unknown, lurking somewhere. Cursing my nerves, I went on scraping with furious dedication. I had barely finished the port side when I was suddenly overwhelmed by an unaccountable desire to look behind. I turned, and as I did so, my heart thumped in mad crescendo—then stopped cold. Hardly twenty yards away, stealthily rising from the depths at an angle of some forty degrees, one of the biggest sharks I have ever seen was coming straight at me, slowly but steadily. The symmetrical tail, streamlined body, unusually long snout and spiky, irregularly protruding teeth were unmistakable. A mako! *

Checking my first, instinctive, impulse to get out of the water, I gripped the knife and flattened myself against the keel. He was too near, and any attempt I made to climb onto *Britannia* would leave my legs dangling for some time, a perfect target for those teeth.

Unexpectedly meeting a shark face to face underwater is a

---

* Mako shark (*Isurus oxyrinchus*). A fully grown mako may measure as much as twelve feet in length and weigh over a thousand pounds. Bluish gray on the back and snow-white below, makos are pelagic sharks, and although they are unquestionably dangerous to man, their primary food is fish (mackerel, tarpon, marlin, etc.). World travelers, they are among the few sharks that qualify as game fishes, jumping out of the water when hooked. They are involved in attacks upon boats more frequently than any other sharks.

harrowing experience, regardless of how many times it may have happened before. Spearfishing and skin diving in the Caribbean had given me my share of encounters with sharks: tigers, bulls, duskies, nurses, hammerheads, great blues—even makos, like this one. From the beginning they had fascinated me, and I had gone to great lengths to study them and observe their behavior. I had finally concluded that 99 percent of sharks will not attack a man unless provoked or otherwise tempted,* that the only sure thing about them is their unpredictability and that pelagic sharks, like the mako, are the most unpredictable of all.

This bastard now—there was a certain something in the leisurely, unwavering determination of his pace as he kept coming straight at me that made me realize he meant business. I gritted my teeth, cursed and waited, completely flat against the boat. There was no time to reason, plan, even be afraid. It simply happened. As the Log reads:

. . . about a foot from me, and my hand was beginning to come down on him with the intention of slashing his nose when he swerved, as if to scratch himself against the boat with me in between. As I said, my knife hand was already about to hit him with all the strength I could muster. Because of his last-moment movement, I missed his nose but caught him right under the mouth, in the soft underbelly. About seven inches of razor-sharp blade went in—and the world exploded in front of me. In a sudden burst of energy the shark pulled away from me and, in doing so, ripped himself open from mouth to tail. I got scraped in the arm and received a terrific blow with the tail on the left shoulder. As the shark sped away, I climbed into Britannia *in record time. Looked round, but did not see shark again. Felt sore and battered but otherwise O.K. One hour later, went back into the*

---

* The great white shark (*Carcharodon carcharias*), a confirmed man-eater, is, possibly, one of the few exceptions.

water to scrape the starboard side. Took me a long time, but finished.
Rowed eight hours.

Here, before I go on, I would like to revise my previous statement that "99 percent of sharks will not attack a man unless provoked or otherwise tempted." Come to think of it, perhaps 80 percent is a slightly more realistic figure. Oh well, life went on, and it was beautiful—really beautiful!

Feb. 22   *33rd day*
Still calm, no wind. Hot. Rowed only five hours, as I feel all sore where the shark's tail hit me. Nothing at all happened.

There was no need for anything to happen. The way I saw it, I had had enough excitement to last me for the rest of the journey. Besides, my left arm and shoulder were in a sorry mess and felt it. Not that I complained. Rather than cause a shark indigestion, my own flesh and bones could go on hurting me as long as they liked. There were other, much better ways, of giving the beggars a bellyache.

"Just you wait till the next one comes around, *Britt*. From now on it's war, and any shark foolish enough to think that your bottom is a plaything to scratch and thump at will is going to receive a surprise or two!"

Feb. 23   *34th day*
Wind from the north, Force 2–3.
Feel better today.
Rowed seven hours.

Feb. 24   *35th day*
Wind from the north, Force 2–3.
Position 24°27′ North, 16°52′ West.
At sunset a Russian ship, the Talsy, *stopped by. Went aboard. Everybody extremely kind. Got some more cans of food and*

*water. I think this will be one of the last ships, as I am about
to get away from the shipping lane. This is good, as all this
time I have been afraid of being run down.*
Rowed nine hours.

With the *Talsy*, Russian ships joined the Norwegians at
the top of my list of ships a castaway ought to look for. Her
captain, Victor Nikitin, also has my respect for the virtuoso
performance of seamanship he displayed while bringing the
Talsy alongside. His judgment and timing were such that
when the *Talsy* stopped, *Britannia* was a mere ten yards
away from the ladder the crew had flung over the side. After
a most pleasurable half hour spent swapping gossip in his
cabin, we had parted in high spirits, greatly helped by half a
bottle of excellent vodka, downed in a spree of toasts that
included the Queen, Lenin, the Royal and Russian navies,
Shakespeare, Tolstoy . . . even ourselves.

As I am not normally a drinking man, it had taken me a
little while to convince *Britannia* that all was well. Unable to
speak her mind, she had shown her disapproval by rolling
and pitching in a most violent and unusual fashion. She had
even gone to the disrespectful extreme of tossing me overboard once or twice, something that had never happened before. All the same, eventually, we returned to the old routine: "In—out. In—out. Tralalalero . . . tralalala. In—out.
In—out. *Figaro qua, Figaro là, Figaro su, Figaro giu. Ehi,
Figaro!* Trala. In—out. In—out."

Singing opera was the best solution I had yet devised to
wile away the drudgery of rowing, choosing the arias according to my mood. Regrettably, the tonal quality never quite
attained the heights I was capable of achieving in my bath-
room. Nevertheless, it was nice to know that my efforts were
unlikely to be vilified by the grunts and moans of a usually
unappreciative audience.

Feb. 25   *36th day*
Calm again. Come on, Venus, make an effort! I need strong
winds from the east. Stop playing about and send them.
Rowed ten hours.

Feb. 26   *37th day*
Wind from the north again, Force 4–5.
This will make me drift south more than I like to, and rowing
is very difficult because waves come from abeam. I really
would like to know whether the trades exist or whether the
whole thing is a bloody myth!
Position at sunset 23° 42′ North, 17° 46′ West.
Rowed ten hours.

Feb. 27 and 28 and Mar. 1   *38th, 39th and 40th days*
I am afraid I did not keep my writing up to date, but anyway, nothing at all happened. Wind still from the north,
Force 3–4.
Another month has gone, and my progress so far is too ridiculous for words. If by the end of March I am not somewhere
between 30° and 35° West Longitude, I will never be able to
reach Florida before the hurricane season. But I will never
do it at this rate!
Position at sunset 23° 00′ North, 18° 54′ West.

Mar. 2 and 3   *41st and 42nd days*
Absolute calm. Sea like a mirror.
Rowed twenty hours.

Mar. 4, 5, 6 and 7   *43rd, 44th, 45th and 46th days*
Sorry about not writing more often, but doggone tired. Wind
has changed at last—has been coming from the east for the
last four days—and I have been rowing twelve hours every
day to try and catch up. Nothing happened, anyway. Winds
Force 1, 2, 3. This always happens with easterly winds, always weak.
Position at sunset 21° 58′ North, 20° 44′ West.

Britannia meets the *Skauborg*.

A shark lassoed alongside *Britannia*.

The same shark, beheaded, surrounded by baby sharks found in her belly.

Mar. 8   *47th day*

Winds from the north, Force 4–5. It was too good to last! Am now rowing northwest. Must try to keep north of Latitude 20°—otherwise it might become impossible to reach Florida. Besides, according to the American Pilot Charts, I will get plenty of winds from the east between Latitudes 20° and 25° and almost none south of that. Rowing on a northwesterly course with the wind from the north is a beastly job, and I am incredibly tired from my four-day twelve-hour attempt. Today I rowed only eight hours; every muscle and bone of my body aches. Britannia weighs tons. To row ten hours daily takes an incredible amount of energy. Am now almost always hungry, in spite of the heat and of eating more than the prescribed amounts; in fact, I am adding a lot of fish (the fried remains of the two dorados I had previously speared) to my daily ration. My water consumption has increased from one gallon every three days to one gallon every two days—this probably because I am rowing more during the daytime than before on account of needing more rest in between rowing spells.

Thanks to the absence of westerly winds, of which I sincerely hoped I had seen the last, the danger of piling up somewhere along the coast of Africa had disappeared, but I was still very unhappy about the way things were going. Already we had drifted far too much to the south in relation to our longitude, and the prospect of ever reaching Florida was beginning to look very bleak indeed. Yet reach Florida we must, and it had to be nonstop! If I failed and arrived in the West Indies or, even worse, someplace in South America, I might still claim, in the eyes of the world, to be the first man to row across the Atlantic single-handed; but in my eyes, and that was all I cared for, I would have failed, miserably. The way I saw it, almost anyone with a good boat, know-how and reasonable perseverance could row across, if that was all he wanted. To me the real challenge was to take *Britannia* to where I had said I would: across the Atlantic *and* to Florida. Anything short of that would not, could not, do. Whatever happened, I knew I would never give up; but at that moment, it seemed so hopeless!

Mar. 9   *48th day*
Wind from the east, Force 1–2. No clouds; very hot.
For some reason, I feel in my bones that the sea is up to something; yet I have no reason to complain at the moment. It must be that I am feeling very sad and depressed today, really blue, for the first time since leaving. Think I need a girl bad. London Traffic is the only female voice I hear when I call London. She's got a beautiful voice, or at least, it seems so out here, and I keep dreaming of her whispering in my ears not "Hello, Britannia" but nice, indescribable things. I have not asked her name yet—sort of want to keep it in mystery—but I think I will ask her next time and invite her to dinner when I return to London. I only hope she is not some old, ugly bitch with a sweet voice. Will I ever go back to London? At this rate it will take me a year to get to Florida.

My last piece of dried fish has gone today. I have not seen a fish for days now. Wonder how in hell Bombard ever managed to catch any and survive. I am following more or less his route, and if I had to depend on fish for food and water, I would have been dead a long time ago. It has rained only twice since I left, a few drops at that.
Rowed ten hours.

Mar. 10   *49th day*
Venus seems to have heard my prayers. Caught a dolphin this morning. Archie has miscalculated the number of calories I need, because I go through his daily ration as if it weren't there. Unless I supplement it with fish or some canned stuff, I remain hungry to the point of feeling weak, without energy for rowing properly. Since my supply of cans is limited, I ab-

solutely need the fish, of which I eat nearly a pound per day
when I have it.
Wind from the northeast, Force 1–2.
Rowed nine hours.

Archie de Jong, Horlicks' nutrition expert, had calculated
that I would need something in the region of three thousand
six hundred kilocalories per day to keep myself in a fit condition. My rations were in one hundred individually sealed
plastic packs, weighing two pounds eight ounces each and
measuring ten inches by four by two. Each pack contained a
one-man/one-day ration, similar to those developed for mili-
tary use, to provide a hot breakfast, cold snack meal and hot
main meal that needed a minimum of preparation and could,
in an emergency, be eaten cold and uncooked. Each of these
one-man/one-day rations consisted of:

Oatmeal block	1	2½-oz. vacuum pack
Holsteiner meat paste (or Spam paste)	1	$2^{13}/_{16}$-oz. tin (tear-opening)
Cheese	1	2-oz. vacuum pack
Materne fruit bars	2	2-oz. envelopes
Enerzade glucose tablets	2	¾-oz. packets
Horlicks tablets	1	¾-oz. packet
Meat/vegetable bar (HF/6 Var.)*	1	2½-oz. vacuum pack
Potato powder *or* rice †	1	2-oz. envelope
Salt	1	½-oz. polythene bag
Biscuits, service	2	3-oz. vacuum packs
Tea bags	2	
Instant skim-milk powder	1	1-oz. envelope
Glucose/lemon–drink powder	1	2-oz. envelope
Horlicks chocolate powder	1	1¼-oz. envelope
Instant coffee	2	envelopes
Sugar	6	cubes

*Three varieties: beef, mutton, steak-and-kidney.
† 45 packs contained potato powder and 45 contained rice.

This was supposed to provide me with a balanced diet and a total of three thousand five hundred and fifty-two kilocalories. So far so good—except that I was supposed to eat exactly the same things, day in, day out, for one hundred days. When, after the first week, my stomach had grasped the full significance of this, it had been appalled by the implications. Thus, whenever the opportunity had presented itself, in the shape of passing ships, I had endeavored to scrounge as great a variety of canned meat and vegetables as possible. Unfortunately, bulk and weight strictly limited the amount I could carry, so I tried to collect a little of as many different items as feasible, in preference to plenty of the most basic.

At this stage I had already reached the point at which opening one of Archie's packs was enough to ruin my mood for an hour or so. For two of his goodies I developed a positive revulsion. I did not dare throw the lot overboard, but these two I did—right away, every day. Somewhat relieved, I would then prepare breakfast—which, almost invariably, consisted of a rather tasty, if sticky, mess of oatmeal, chocolate and milk powder and biscuits, crumbled and diluted in a pint of boiling water. The rest I ate whenever I felt hungry, which could be almost any time of day or night. My most precious treasures were a bagful of assorted spices and a few onions (a Russian present!). All my cooking was done in a pressure cooker, but I had used it as such only a few times. Finding the results less than satisfactory, I soon dispensed with the lid and went on cooking in normal, everyday fashion. A thick soup of chopped-up dorado head, onion and rice, liberally sprinkled with black pepper, was my favorite dish at the time.

Mar. 11   *50th day*
This is beautiful. For the first time in ages, wind from the northeast, Force 4–5. It is what I need, and if it keeps like this for a week or two I should start making some decent

progress. However, I'll never be able to recover all the time lost, and even with the best of luck, it will be impossible for me to arrive in Florida before the end of June. This if I can make an average of thirty miles per day—which, in the light of what has happened so far, I must regard as nearly impossible.
Rowed ten hours.

Mar. 12   *51st day*
Wind from the northeast, Force 4–5.
Position at sunset 20°50′ North, 22°58′ West.
Rowed ten hours.

Comparing my position with that of March 7, I realized that northeasterly winds were not so good after all; in fact, as far as Florida was concerned, they were not good at all. In the last six days our progress westward had been one hundred and thirty-four nautical miles—an average of twenty-two miles per day. But in spite of my efforts, our drift south had continued, so that we had lost another degree of latitude. Gaining two degrees of longitude at the expense of one degree of latitude would never do.

"Do you realize what we are up against, *Britt*? We have come so far south that the trades are no longer good for us. We have reached a stage at which only easterly winds can save us. What chances do you think we have?"

She did not know the answer, but I did. None. A quick inspection of the Log showed that so far, in fifty days, we had had six days of westerly winds, eleven of southwesterlies, two and a half of southeasterlies, seven and a half of easterlies, nine of northeasterlies, seven of northerlies, three of northwesterlies and five days calm. On only ten days, out of fifty, had the winds blown from the, for us, right quarter. With over three thousand miles to go, Florida had never seemed so far.

"It is hopeless, *Britt*. Utterly hopeless. We might as well give up and content ourselves with just crossing the Atlantic, whatever our landfall at the other side may turn out to be."

Give up? Just like that? It was sensible, the only sensible thing to do. What did it matter if we could not reach Florida? Why Florida, anyway? Just because I had said we would. So what?

Had the winds been northeasterlies from the beginning, as they were supposed to be, we would probably have been over halfway across the Atlantic by now. In theory we should have been able to complete the journey in three and a half months, four at most. If only the winds had been right! But they hadn't, and now, after fifty-one days at sea, our westerly progress was only four hundred and twenty miles (an incredibly poor average of slightly over eight miles per day), and we were three hundred miles *south* of our intended course. These were the cold, stark, realistic figures that no amount of wishful thinking could change. We had fought and, I think, fought bravely. What more was there that one could do, that one had not already done? In fact, things looked so bad that if I had any sense left, I should not only forget Florida, but steer *Britannia* to the Cape Verde Islands, some two hundred and forty miles south of our present position, and start afresh, if at all. Now, while the north and northeasterly winds still made it possible. A few more days and we would pass the point of no return. Once we were to the west of the Cape Verdes, we would be committed. Whatever happened afterward, there could be no regrets, no turning back. The trades would make sure of that. The tousled expanse of the Atlantic would be there, facing us at its widest, ready to engage in a battle that, for the Atlantic, had not yet started. Shall we go on, regardless of the consequences, or turn back? It was an agonizing decision to make, with no margin for error, but I had to make it, entirely on my own, today.

Too tired to think straight, I lashed the oars and attempted to find sleep and inspiration in my rathole. Neither came, as my brain, a turmoil of thoughts and memories, refused to either concentrate or go blank. Strange how, sometimes, the images and feelings of the past come back, as vivid as when it all had happened—seven, eight years before?

I was squatting on the foul-smelling deck of one of Captain Z.'s fishing boats, beheading shrimps with my naked, bleeding fingers, the slimy, inexhaustible mountain, fresh from the sea, a blurred vision in front of my eyes.

Captain Z.—sailor, adventurer *extraordinaire*, the man who had taken me under his wing and, with brutal, no-nonsense affection, was determined, someday, to make a trusted lieutenant out of me: but only if I had what it took, and learned the painful, untrimmed truths of what a real soldier of fortune's life was all about. After a few months of navigation training on one of his fast boats, carrying cargo up and down the Caribbean, he had decided the time had come for a further step in my development.

"We shall go out in one of my shrimp trawlers," he had said smoothly.

Fishing shrimps! If I have ever hated anything in my life, this was it. Once we were on the fishing ground, the net had to be hauled up every two hours, day and night—which meant that no one could have more than two hours' uninterrupted sleep. In practice, if and when the catch was big, not even that, because the shrimps had to be beheaded one by one, thousands of them, and stored, and the deck cleared for the next haul. After two days of this, the tips of my fingers were completely raw and I couldn't touch anything, let alone behead a shrimp. The Captain allowed me half a day to rest, then ordered me back to work. He was out to kill me—or, as he put it, "I'll make a man out of you or bust you." Well, I was bust. But he wouldn't hear of it and drove me twice as hard as any of the fishermen who had never done anything else all their lives. I was his favorite, and the price I had to pay was to prove myself to his satisfaction. There was no arguing with him, either; when he wanted something, whether for a reason or just for kicks, he got it, and that was that.

After a five-day, almost nonstop spell of frenzied working, we ran out of sewing cord for maintaining the nets and decided to buy or borrow some from the next shrimp boat we came upon. When one did appear, the Captain was sleeping and I was at the wheel. Rather than disturb him, I went alongside the other boat and hollered my request. They did have spare cord, so I went in nearer, coming up from astern of them. The sea was dead calm, and all I wanted was to get close enough alongside for them to throw us a ball or two of cord. As simple a maneuver as there can be—except, perhaps, that I was too worn out, mentally and physically, to know what I was doing. The next thing I knew, I had failed to calculate correctly the speed of my boat, the speed of the other boat and, more particularly, the length of a boom they had swinging over the side, and all hell was about to break loose. It did.

I went full astern, but it was too late. Inexorably we plowed on and into the boom—which came straight in, shearing off most of our wheelhouse like a knife taking the froth off beer and, as I flattened myself on deck, nearly impaling me in the process. I had started to get up, only to dive again as our propeller caught hold of the water and we went astern, shaking free of the boom—which, on its way out, removed what little was left of the bridge.

The Captain had come storming up to find me still lying on deck, covered with wood splinters, glass and bits of charts. Arms akimbo, stark naked, actually trembling with rage, he had surveyed the mess, cutting such an extraordinary figure that, in my hysterical fear over what had happened and what was going to happen, I could almost have laughed. Unbelievably, he must have been so stunned that such an occurrence could have happened to his bridge that he didn't say anything. He just looked at me and, God! I wished I had been a thousand miles away. When he finally spoke, rather tightly, brushing aside my mumbled explanations, I could hardly believe my ears:

"O.K., Johnny, go get some sleep. We'll talk about this later."

In a half daze, I had stumbled to my bunk, clambered into it and spent the next ten hours deeply asleep. That I had been allowed to sleep that long, and could, was a measure of my exhaustion.

At the postmortem, the Captain, after hearing me out, had said with great calm, although I could see that it was an effort:

"It will cost about two hundred dollars to put right the damage. You will pay for it. Three times. Once for being stupid. Twice because you made a mistake and must pay for it. And the third time so that you will remember."

Remember? How could I ever forget it? He had made me pay to the last cent. What a man! Hard as nails: only nails will bend; he wouldn't. He had given me the most exciting times of my life, and I had never known what thrills the next day would bring. I simply lived through every one as if it were my last—which, with him ruling them out for me, might well have been so. But there was something else about that fishing trip I will never forget. The unbearable pain of beheading shrimp after shrimp with my raw fingers and the sneering remarks that had prodded me to go on, out of pride, to the end of physical endurance were meant to have a purpose.

When I had finished paying the last $200, the ones I was to pay to remember, the Captain had told me:

"What I wanted you to learn, Johnny, is that one always pays for one's mistakes, whatever they are. You crashed into that boat because your judgment was clouded, as you were on the verge of exhaustion; but knowing so, you should not have tried any fancy maneuvers—especially at sea, where a man never knows what may happen to him; he must always be able to know, regardless of his condition, what he can or cannot do. As for beheading shrimps with your bleeding fingers, that should teach you that as long as you have a will to drive you on, there is no such thing in life as giving up something you have to do just because it proves to be painful or difficult."

The Captain's motto had been "Never give up."

Never give up! In the four years I had spent with him, these words had been imprinted on my mind in blood, sweat and tears. The Captain's parting words had been "I have made half a man out of you. The other half you must make yourself. But whatever you do, remember, never, never give up."

Crawling out of my rathole, I gave *Britannia* a playful kick, then sat down and manned the oars. There was, after all, no need for me to think what I was going to do anymore. The decision had been made for me long ago: seven, eight years before.

7

Mar. 13   52nd day
Wind from the north, Force 2–3.
*Got through to London and had a word with Sylvia. This has
cheered me up a bit. Also asked Noel Botham to get in touch
with the American Coast Guard and see if they can offer any
advice as to my chances of reaching Florida provided I can
make it to 60° West Longitude by the end of May. I am sure
their answer will be negative, but we shall see.*
*Got another dolphin today, right after seeing him catch
two flying fish. In fact, I caught him for this reason only.
The flying fish were in his stomach, still nearly alive, and I
fried them with my last onion—delicious! Also, since March
10 I have had a companion—another dorado, whom I can
easily recognize because he has a scar on his back. This one
seems to have adopted us, and I feed him the scraps from the*

*other dorados. I call him Jerrycan. Wonder for how long he
is going to follow us?*
Rowed ten hours.

Jerrycan was the male companion to the fish whose head
had made such a tasty soup on the tenth (I knew his sex
because male dorados have a blunt, almost square head,
whereas the females have more delicate lines). He was
slightly over average size—about four and a half feet long
and, probably, around the forty-pound mark. He had been
spared the pot because I had more than enough with the female, and now the new arrival would give me all the meat I
could possibly use for some time. Cut in long, thin strips, it
takes only about three days to dry, after which it can keep
indefinitely. Another reason I am sparing Jerrycan is that if I
continue to feed him, his presence is likely to attract other
dorados—who, if they get used to our company and follow
us the same way they followed Bombard's raft, will then be a
ready supply of fresh fish, always at hand.

Mar. 14   *53rd day*
*It was too good to last. Today the wind is from the north-
northwest, Force 4–5. This will make me drift even more to
the south, as I cannot now row on a northwesterly course as
I was doing. Now I'll probably lose one degree of latitude for
every degree of longitude I gain.*
*Also, my behind is very sore. For the first, I have a rash,
and sitting while rowing is becoming very painful. Rubbed it
with surgical alcohol. Hope it will pass.*
Rowed ten hours.

For nearly a month now I had been dispensing with
clothes and spending most of the time stark naked. This had
been made possible by an increasingly warm temperature,
wavering between 37° Centigrade in the daytime and 30°
Centigrade at night.*

    * 98.7° and 86° Fahrenheit.

To be naked not only gave my movements a wonderful sense of freedom but also gave me a beautiful overall tan. *Britannia* being an open boat with only ten inches' freeboard, it was most unusual for an hour to go by without everything's being soaked in a shower of spray. While this was undoubtedly inconvenient, it did not matter greatly as far as equipment was concerned, as everything I wanted to keep dry was, more or less permanently, stowed in the eight watertight compartments belowdecks, or, like the generator, safely wrapped in waterproof canvas, and, *Britannia* being self-bailing, any water shipped in found its own way out within seconds. It was different where *I* was concerned. To be warm and dry and suddenly have a bucketful of cold water thrown at one is not very pleasant, to say the least. Those who have been selected for similar charming jokes while sunbathing on a beach will know what I mean—bearing in mind that I was usually not relaxing but doggone tired, with nerves stretched to the limit by lack of sleep and in a mood of general frustration at the way things were going. I find it hard to remember anything during the entire journey I cursed more feelingly than these repetitive and not-so-harmless pranks of the sea. So far, by staying naked as much as possible, I had avoided the rashes so common at sea, usually caused by the chafing of clothes against soft, waterlogged skin. That the first one should appear on my buttocks was unavoidable. If anything, the amazing thing was that it had taken so long.

My sliding seat, which was of wood, was a perfect fit, and I had a small cushion of foam on it—perhaps not such a good idea after all. The friction caused by sitting and sliding back and forth for hours on end, sweat and salt water constantly trickling down my spine, was bound to cause irritation. Since I could not stop rowing, now that it had started chances were that it would go on getting worse, and I wondered how bad that would be. Already I had the feeling, while rowing, that somebody was, industriously if still gently, rubbing the inside of my buttocks with a strip of finely grained sand-paper. Placing a cotton vest on top of the foam cushion was, for the time being, the only palliative I could think of.

Mar. 15   *54th day*
Wind from the northeast, Force 2, 3, 1, variable.
Better than yesterday—but I wonder why the winds that are more favorable to me are always so weak.
My Ronson lighter stopped working today. Slowly but re-lentlessly, the sea is beginning to leave its print on everything, and I discovered that I have no matches. Sylvia* bought some supposedly special, waterproof ones in Las Palmas—but she doesn't speak Spanish, and God knows what they understood she wanted. The first one exploded in my hand. The second one shot away all over Britannia *in a shower of sparks and finished in the sea. The third simply went* pouff! *in a cloud of stinking smoke. They are little petards for fire-works displays, and they won't light the Calor gas! Threw the lot away in disgust and sat down to repair the Ronson. Thanks to my lucky stars, it's working again. This may seem humorous—and indeed, I can't help smiling when I imagine poor Sylvia shopping in Spanish—but the end result may well be a rather tragic one for me and cause me endless troubles, if not worse. The Ronson is now the only means I have of making fire. Without it I cannot cook, and—what is really worrying me—I cannot make drinking water. Am not in the shipping lanes anymore, and the nearest to me is at least a month away. I shan't reach it till about 40°–35° West Longi-tude, depending on my latitude. My position is now 20°30′ North, 24° West, approximately. Thus, if anything happens to the Ronson I will be in most serious trouble. I have seven gallons of water left—fourteen days' supply; the rest I must*

---

* Sylvia is most indignant at this and strongly denies being responsible for the purchase of matches! Must have been another non–Spanish-speaking member of our shopping expeditions.

distill. I will do this now and leave what I have as standby for emergencies. Once I get into the shipping lanes, I must see and stop a ship at all costs, however, and get some matches. This is a ridiculous thing to have happen—and, of course, entirely my fault, as I should have checked before leaving. Still, it is no use crying over spilt milk. One thing I promise: if that lighter doesn't give up, I will never again in my life use anything but a Ronson.
Becalmed.
Rowed ten hours.

The Cape Verde Islands were now only one hundred and eighty miles due south of us: our last chance of seeking safe harbor before irrevocably committing ourselves to cross the Atlantic in whatever condition we had been reduced to by fifty-four days of incessant combat against the sea. Not that it mattered much as far as *Britannia* was concerned. She was in as good shape as she would ever be in. For me it was different. The remorseless bite of the elements was beginning to leave its mark on my physical condition. The same could be said of the equipment. While in this there was nothing serious yet, the unpalatable truth was that nearly two months had been lost and, our being so far south, there was the same distance between us and Florida as there had been the day we left San Agustín. If our chances had been slim before, what were they now?

The discovery that I had no matches was a hard blow, not because without them I could not cook (my rations could be eaten raw in an emergency, and so could fish) but, as I noted in the Log, because my water supplies depended on my ability to make fire. In my condition, a week without water would be the most I could hope to survive—and whatever else I may be, I am not suicide-minded. What guarantee could I have that, having failed once, the lighter would not pack up for good?

Lack of fresh water has always been the greatest problem of survival at sea. A problem that, in my case, could not have been solved in a better way. With the hundred and eighty disposable containers supplied by Calor Gas, I had enough fuel to make forty-five gallons of drinking water. The procedure was as simple as it was effective. I had two pressure cookers—one for cooking, the other for distilling seawater. The moment the water started boiling, the steam would leave the pressure cooker through a specially adapted valve in the lid and continue through two yards of flexible hose to the condenser coils. These were of half-inch copper tubing mounted in a rectangular steel frame, roughly twelve inches by eight by three, which could be clamped to the gunwale, where the coils were cooled by the wind. I would collect the steady trickle of tepid, tasteless water in a plastic jerry can held beneath the coils. Thus, in five hours, using two canisters of Calor gas, I was able to produce half a gallon of chemically pure distilled water. All I had to do during the entire process was keep an occasional eye on the burner and replace the empty gas canister. With a ten-to-one ratio (I could make ten pounds of water with one pound of gas), its advantage, from a rower's point of view, hardly needs stressing. This method was ideal, provided I could make fire; otherwise I would be in trouble.

According to my Pilot Charts, there were only two shipping lanes between our present position and the West Indies, and these would cross our route more or less at right angles. The first one, New York to the Cape of Good Hope, was nearly a thousand miles away, and the second, New York to the east coast of South America, about eight hundred miles farther west. These were the roughly measured distances, provided we could reach them along our present latitude— that is to say, 20° North. Even so, getting there was one thing, being spotted quite another. If we went on, I would be staking my life on the assumption that my lighter would go

on working, and what reason did I have to suppose it would?
Except that it was MADE IN ENGLAND, none whatever.

Mar. 16   *55th day*
Wind from the northeast, Force 3–4.
My rash is not getting any better, and rowing is slowly be-
coming something of a Chinese torture. Just to think about
what it will feel like the moment I start rowing seems almost
as painful as the actual thing. Oh well, live and endure.
Rowed nine hours.

I forgot to say that in the afternoon of the preceding day,
just before I paid my compliment to British industry by deciding to go on, a school of dorados had joined Jerrycan, and
we now had company. They were about fifty, possibly more,
and their presence cheered me up no end. Going overboard,
the better to introduce myself, I was soon on friendly terms
with the majority of them. The excitement of having a new
fish in their midst was matched only by their curiosity. On
several occasions they came so near that I was able to touch
them with my hand, upon which they would dart away, only
to return a few seconds later, more curious than ever. Back
on board, I fed them with the bits and pieces of the previous
dorados, and now, after spearing a couple of the newcomers,
I did the same. They fed as if in a frenzy, and often several of
them whooshed toward the same bait at the same time, from
opposite directions. The result was then a multiple, head-on
collision of terrific violence, leaving the lot momentarily
dazed. Cunning, usually much smaller, ones would then
pounce on the opportunity and make a mad dash for it,
squeezing themselves in between their stunned brothers and
smartly getting away with the prize.
I also noticed that Jerrycan, whether out of resentment toward the new arrivals or because he considered the feeding
habits of the populace beneath his dignity, never mixed with

them, patiently waiting for his share right alongside *Britannia*. I liked that, as it meant that other dorados might, conceivably, adopt a similar attitude, considering *Britannia* a source of food and friendship, rather than death. Jerrycan had been with us for six days by this time, and showed no inclination to leave, so maybe the possibilities of a floating larder permanently at my disposal were not so farfetched after all.

"As long as we go on feeding them regularly, *Britt*, I don't think they will bother to think about the implications."

Mar. 17   56th day
Wind from the north, Force 4–5.
Today I took a rest. Rowed only four hours. I just had to give attention to that bloody rash. Rubbed it with surgical alcohol every half hour, then put my bottom to the sun. At the end of the day—that is, now—I feel much better. It seems to have dried almost completely. Considering that in three days' time it will be two months since our departure and that this is the first time I am bugged by a physical ailment—my back injury at the beginning was more in the nature of an accident—I think that's one department at least in which I have been lucky, and I congratulate myself on what still is, generally, a splendid physical condition. However, my behind and my hands are the very worst places to have anything wrong with, and I do hope this rash will eventually go. My hands, by the way, are keeping up very well, which is due, I think, to the fact that my oars keep at right angles to the water and I do not have to feather or strain my hands in any way; all I do is push or pull, which reduces the rubbing to a minimum. Also, I wear gloves most of the time.
Position 19°57′ North, 24°35′ West.

Mar. 18   57th day
Completely calm all day—not a puff of wind. Very hot, 35°C. Because of this, could row only early morning and evening.

Very good for my bottom. Kept up the same treatment; getting better all the time.
Rowed six hours.

These were the sort of days when nothing at all could be done. Thirty-five degrees Centigrade (in the shade) may not sound all that much, but in the absence of wind and clouds, the heat was truly hellish. As for my sleeping quarters, underneath the forward self-righting chamber, I did not call them a "rathole" for nothing. The available space was six feet in length by two feet high—barely enough for me to crawl under. An oven, if there was no breeze. A one-man Beauford life raft had been my bunk. I had kept it inflated at all times —not so much to have it ready in case of emergency, but rather for its far more practical use as a mattress and pillow. Alas, gone were the days when, after hours of slaving at the oars, I could look forward to lying in soft, cozy abandon on a cushion of air. Remember the day of my fireworks display? That second petard, the one that had gone wild all over *Britannia* before dying in the sea—well, damn it all, apparently only half had gone overboard; the other half had settled on the Beauford, leaving a souvenir the size of a soccer ball, and my beautiful bed was now a tangled mass of stinking rubber. The only reason I kept it was to spite *Britannia.* I know, as sure as that her deck was all my weary bones now had to lie on, that she had engineered the whole thing. The unspeakable bitch either was jealous, or resented the implication of mistrust of her seaworthiness hinted at by the presence of a life raft. That's the trouble with small boats: the moment you show a bit of affection they start thinking they own you. Give them a finger and they will take your arm. Next she will start saying she wants a new coat of paint, or maybe that her bottom could do with some more scratching. "Well, you won't get either. I am far more interested in my own bottom at the moment." Gosh, but it was hot! The afternoon seemed to drag on forever.

Mar. 19   *58th day*
Wind from the north, Force 2–3.
Jerrycan is still around and getting fat at my expense. Think
he has given up fishing on his own altogether, because he is
never more than a few yards away from Britannia, *whether I*
am rowing or not.

The other dolphins had remained in our company as well, and this day we all had a marvelous time dispatching a hammerhead shark.

It was early afternoon, and I was contemplating going over the side for a swim. Half an hour's swimming was something I indulged in almost every day. It was my way of relaxing, mentally as well as physically—like going for a stroll in the park, so to speak, but spiced by the prickly awareness of latent danger. But I was not careless about it. Either with the drogue attached if the wind was not favorable, as now, or free, I always made sure that *Britannia* had at least a hundred feet of warp trailing behind, and I never went into the water without my flippers, mask and knife. Swimming with flippers, I had found that even in a Force 6 wind I could easily outpace *Britannia*'s drift, and the mask allowed me to keep an eye on the surroundings. Even so, I never strayed more than, at most, twenty yards from *Britannia*, usually keeping upwind of her so that, if necessary, in a burst of speed I could cover this distance in a matter of seconds.

Not that I would have tried to in the unlikely event of a shark's catching me again with my pants down. In such cases it is best to swim with steady, regular strokes, preferably underwater. A shark's pattern of attack is usually very cautious, with the shark keeping a prudent distance, circling in a lazy, seemingly unconcerned way, occasionally making a slow, diffident pass at the intended victim. When sharks know they have been noticed, this is their general behavior where humans are concerned, as is borne out by my own personal observations in many encounters with sharks, both in the Caribbean and in the Pacific off Panama and the Pearl Islands. I have also had the unpleasant experience of spearing a fish only to have it snatched away from the spear by what can only be called a lightning attack, as fast as those I have witnessed of sharks running down free-swimming fish. What causes them to change their tactics when attacking human beings I don't know, but they do.

My scrap with the mako has done nothing to change my mind in this respect, as his approach, while unusually direct, had also been extremely slow. For that matter, I am not even positively sure that the mako's intention had been that of attacking me, and not of simply scratching himself against *Britannia* with me accidentally in between. Unfortunately, very little is known still about sharks, and while there are several theories as to what the swimmer's or skin diver's best course of action should be if he is unlucky enough to be attacked by a shark, there are no cut-and-dried rules. No shark can be relied on to behave in the same manner as another, and it is often difficult to judge whether an approaching shark is attacking rather than just being curious. The safest course is to consider all approaching sharks as attacking ones. My own strategy in such cases is to dive and swim straight at them. This has always resulted in the shark's turning on his tail and thereafter keeping at a safe distance, giving me the opportunity to get out of the water if I consider it dangerous not to do so.

After scanning the sea and duly convincing myself that all was as it should be, I had one foot on the gunwale and was about to dive when something caught my attention out of the corner of my eye.

Was it or wasn't it? Turning to have a better look, I could not see anything, yet I was sure a black speck had momentarily flickered in the blue, somewhere a hundred yards away. Driftwood? Why, then, could I not see it anymore? Visibility was excellent, there was no swell and a gentle, northerly breeze barely ruffled the sea. All around, the water was a clear, pure sapphire, alive with the pranks of my dolphins as they chased one another. A beautiful, perfect day for a swim. What was I waiting for? A last glance at the drogue to see that it was still doing its job properly and, "Watch it boys, here I come!"

Just before going under, I saw it again. A glimpse, but this time unmistakable. A huge, dark triangle was cleaving the surface right over the drogue.

The air bubbles created by my plunging body were still rising when I was back on board, looking hard, but again the elusive, unwelcome visitor was nowhere to be seen. Except for the school of dolphins now swimming in compact formation right under *Britannia*, everything was as it had been. No clue there as to what was going on, as they always behaved in the same way, coming up in a closed bunch to have a look at me every time I jumped overboard.

As long as I stayed on *Britannia*, I couldn't have cared less if one or a hundred sharks fancied playing hide-and-seek in the depths below. After all, it was their sea. What I did resent was the timing. I was having my daily five-hour afternoon break, it was too hot to sleep and, damn it, I felt like swimming! But without knowing who the bugger was, I did not dare. Could be a great white for all I knew, and that's a fellow in whose company I would not swim if I were offered the crown jewels. So, who and where is it?

Finally, I spotted it again. A shark no doubt, but still too far away for identification. A monster all the same, judging by the size of the fin. Why didn't he come near? The mushrooming patch of the drogue seemed to attract him more than anything else. To tempt him nearer, I started pulling in the drogue, and sure enough, he followed it. Followed and swallowed!—with a jerk that sent me reeling before I could let go of the warp. He spat it out almost immediately and

swam away, but not before I recognized him. The character-
istic odd, flat shape of the head was unmistakable. A hammerhead! * Immediately I set about clearing the deck for
battle.

A hammerhead's head makes a beautiful trophy, and I was
determined to grace *Britannia* with this one's. Half an hour
passed by and he was still circling around; but it was obvious
that unless I managed to lure him, he would never come near
—and I needed him to come right alongside *Britannia* to pass
my lasso around his head. Tempting him with big chunks of
a dolphin I had speared and was keeping to feed my boys
later on produced no results other than to work him up into a
state of frenzied excitement. Assuming it was *their* feeding
time, my boys fearlessly dashed in and grabbed the juicy bits
almost before they touched the water. In spite of his efforts,
the relatively cumbersome giant was invariably left gawking,
his cavernous mouth ludicrously snapping at naught.
Mobbed from all sides, looking a silly dotard as he fruitlessly
rushed about, the poor thing suddenly went berserk and, instead of going for the chunky piece I had just landed in front
of his silly head, sped after the biggest of his tormentors.
What a sight!

In what seemed a fantastic surge of speed, they both shot
off: the dolphin a flash of blue lightning—jumping, skimming the top of the waves—and hot on his tail, touching it
almost—matching every twist, every zigzag—the dark, awesome dorsal fin, cleaving the surface in a blur of seemingly
inescapable doom.

"Don't let him catch you, boy. Don't let the beggar get
away with it!"

---

* Smooth hammerhead shark (*Sphyrna zygaena*). Front margin of head is
convex, not indented in the midline. Back dark olive-gray or brownish color;
paler to white below. Maximum length 13–14 feet. Nearly worldwide; ex-
tends into cool waters more than any other species of hammerhead. One of
the strongest swimmers of all sharks, forever on the lookout for anything that
might constitute food. Confirmed man-eater.

The mad chase went on in ever-widening circles. Then back they came, heading straight for *Britannia*, faster, faster —*whoosh!* Leaping out of the water, the dolphin had gone right over *Britannia*, safely plunging back on the other side with a tremendous splash, while the hammerhead, once more outclassed and outsmarted, admitted defeat by swerving away ten yards short of her.

After that I wanted to catch him more than ever.

Lamentably, since he still persisted in keeping out of range, a small sacrifice on the part of the dorados was necessary. I chose as the most suitable a medium-sized female and, as she swam by, shot her through the gills. Immediately she started thrashing, tingeing the water with a fast-spreading cloud of blood. This proved such an irresistible stimulus to the unsated, grievously tantalized maw of the hammerhead that, throwing caution to the winds, he lunged at the writhing dorado with such abandon that I don't think he ever saw the open loop of my lasso dangling in front. Once the incongruous head had gone through, there was no hope for him. Swallowing all but the head of the dolphin in a single, gargantuan gulp, he sounded, in a deep, headlong dive—to be suddenly checked by the rope; then pulled, with such massive strength that for a moment, I thought the half-inch nylon would snap.

The hammerhead was five long, desperately agonizing minutes gasping his way to Hades, but get there he did—and good riddance!

Brought aboard, he proved a full ten feet long. It took me over an hour to chop him up into pieces small enough for my boys to swallow; but to watch their zestful joy as they gorged themselves was more than worth it. The head and fins I kept for myself.

Mar. 20   *59th day*
Wind from the north, Force 5–6.
Blast it all! Very wet day and, naturally, must have drifted

*south quite a bit. Rash almost gone. Two months today since
departure. Feeling fine and in excellent spirits.
Rowed ten hours.*

Usually I took sightings only once every three days, either
at dusk or at dawn. A three- or four-star fix would then give
me our position right away. For a few days it was all I
needed as, for the time being, all my interest was centered on
steering *Britannia* on a broad westerly course, while attempting to lose as little latitude as possible. In between, I was
perfectly satisfied to guess our position, seldom erring by
more than thirty, or at most, forty, miles. If this sounds a lot,
it must be remembered that navigation by esteem* is based
on an accurate knowledge of course, speed and leeway, all of
which were impossible to assess with certainty from a rowing
boat. For this reason, unless I was particularly interested in
knowing my latitude (irrespective of longitude), I never
bothered with the time-honored operation of shooting the
sun at its meridian (noon), in spite of its relative simplicity
compared with other sightings. In celestial, as in coastal,
navigation, a single observation will give a position line only.
The navigator will then know he is somewhere on the line,
but not where he is along it. At least two observations, giving
position lines that cross, are required for a fix.

Mar. 21   *60th day*
Wind from the northeast, Force 3–4.
*Jerrycan bit my finger today. Luckily, it is only a scratch. I
was washing a spoon over the side and he probably thought
it was a bit of fish—greedy little bastard! The other boys are
great fun to watch and a relief from the monotony. The water
is so clear it is like being on top of an aquarium. Their incredible speed allows them to follow the schools of flying fish
(of which there are many to be seen now), matching their
speed in the air underwater and catching them at the end of*

* Dead reckoning.

*their flight—most times, anyway. I do hope they stay with us
for some time.*
*I am getting bored and wish a storm would come from the
east to speed us along and liven things up.*
Rowed ten hours.

Mar. 22   *61st day*
*Of all things—wind from the northwest, Force 4–5! Blew like
that all day and night. This kind of wind is not supposed to
be around here at all. Nevertheless . . . Hope it will stop tonight. One of the water bags leaked, and I found out only
today. So instead of seven gallons, I have only two gallons
left. In case of emergency I could make it last, rationing myself, six days at most, if I am to go on rowing. I am really
keeping my fingers crossed, because if something happens to
that Ronson . . .*
*Getting short of tobacco as well. Am now smoking one cigar,
five cigarettes and one pipe per day. Maybe it will last till we
reach the shipping lane.*
Very tired. Rowed ten hours.

Mar. 23   *62nd day*
Wind still from the northwest, Force 4–5, mostly 5.
*It's a beastly job to row against it, and by now I know exactly
what it is like to be a galley slave.*
*The position at dusk was 19°10′ North, 26° West. At sunset of
the twenty-first it was 19°30′ North, 26° West. Two days of
northwesterlies and all I have managed is to lose twenty miles
of latitude. What bloody luck! I have been steering northwest
since March 1, in the hope of making west; instead I am going
southwest—a difference of ninety degrees between what I
steer and what I actually make good. Unless I can alter this
I cannot see how, the way things are going, we can possibly
make it to Florida. Am beginning to think we will not even
reach the West Indies; at this rate the most we can hope for
is to arrive at Georgetown, Guyana. It is quite obvious to me*

now that, at least at this latitude, it is almost impossible for a single man to row a boat on his desired course. The drift to the south is too fast. Two men could, probably, by taking turns to keep the boat moving most of the time—twenty hours out of twenty-four, anyway. They would not stop drifting, but their westerly progress would be much faster. Even so, I guess they would have one hell of a job. Well, I am on my own and have no regrets whatsoever about that. If anything, I would like a girl to be around, preferably Sylvia; but that's a wishful thinking. I can only go on and row, row, row . . .

Ten hours again, and I am as good as dead.

Mar. 24   63rd day

Can't believe it, but there it is: wind from the northwest, Force 5–6. How the hell is one supposed to go on like this? What have I done to you, Venus, and all the gods alike, to deserve this? And ITN had the unbelievable cheek to ask, this morning, what do I do with my spare time! Spare time? By Jove don't they realize what it is like out here? I row ten hours, almost every day. When I don't it's because, like today, I'm too damn tired to grasp an oar, let alone pull it and move a ton of boat against the wind. I am navigator, cook, deckhand, engine, photographer, radioman: you name, I got to do it— who else? A storm could hit us without warning, so Britannia must be kept shipshape at all times. A day has twenty-four hours. I get up at 0500 GMT (0300 zone time); by 1200 GMT I have rowed five hours; a break until 1700 GMT and then row another five hours, till 2400 GMT—when I go, drop rather, to sleep till 0500 GMT and start again. Thus I sleep five hours in a row. I wake up every hour or two, but never mind. If I can, I catch another hour of sleep after midday. This leaves about eight hours when, in theory, I could do other things. In practice, I cannot row without resting in between, and this takes care of another two to three hours, during which I am too busy, just lying down to get my breath back, to do anything. And then I have to do every-thing else, as mentioned. Spare time? If I catch a dolphin every now and then, it's not for sport but because I need it, and it is bloody—literally—work, as dolphins are big and strong and jolly good fighters. It takes me an hour to clean up from beginning to end. No matter what one does, every-thing takes three to four times as long as it should on Britan-nia because she is so cramped, wet, rolling without pause, slippery . . . Spare time? If I can squeeze out any, I kill a shark if there are any around—hate the bastards! Might end up inside one of them in the near future, and I want to make sure that if that happens, I have good company.

Rowed eight hours; steered west; could not cope against the wind any longer. Fagged out.

This description, written in a moment of angered indigna-tion, will perhaps give an idea of what my days were like. Day after day, with nothing to do but row—rest—row.

The worst thing, perhaps, was getting up. The alarm clock would go off right inside my brain, shrilling, screaming, shat-tering every single cell, on and on . . . then, suddenly, stop; and I would lie there, a wretched bundle of aching flesh and bones, eyes wide open, mesmerized by the white ceiling of Plastazote a foot or so from my nose, thinking—no, not thinking: for a while I could not think, imagine even, only feel. The agony of crawling out, of facing another day the same, row—rest—row . . . And what for? I was not even winning: inch by inch, Florida was retreating farther and farther beyond a horizon I could not dream of touching, not anymore.

8

On March 25, my sixty-fourth day, I crossed the Rubicon. A gamble, perhaps one of the greatest gambles of my life; but I played my cards in a reasoned, dispassionate way—or so I liked to think.

There was no doubt in my mind that as far as crossing the Atlantic was concerned, I would succeed; but getting simply *anywhere* on the other side meant nothing, less than nothing, to me. As I saw it, the supreme challenge, the only possible justification for the pathos of my struggle against adversity and the only way I would ever know that I, and not the sea, had emerged the victor was to take *Britannia* to where I had said I would. To Florida.

The wind had changed. Today, at last, it blew from the east, Force 4–5. The time had come to revise my strategy, lick my wounds and start afresh.

Britannia was heavy, far too heavy. I had had food for

three and a half months, nearly three hundred pounds in weight. Burning energy at the rate of four thousand calories per day, I needed every ounce of it, and the nearest shipping lane, New York to the Cape of Good Hope, was slightly over eight hundred miles to the west of us. Could we make it in a month? Suppose I dropped overboard all the surplus food, leaving only enough for this month. Could I rely on getting there in time? And, what was more, on being sighted by a ship? Of course not! In which case I would have to depend on fish alone to survive. I might find enough to survive, but not enough to go on rowing: I would soon become too weak for that. Still, if I could gain half a knot by lightening *Britannia,* and row twelve hours instead of ten—I had given up too soon in my previous attempt and had not gone about it in a methodical way—our daily average could be increased by ten to fifteen miles. We were doing twenty, twenty-five miles now, so that would bring it up to thirty, thirty-five miles; maybe, with a wind like today's, even forty—double! Also, there were plenty of things I could do without. The big If was whether a lighter *Britannia* would respond to the oars and increase her speed by as much as I calculated. Would she? There was only one way to find out.

. . . done! The die is cast. I left food for thirty days only. If my boys stay around, I can always go on indefinitely on a diet of dolphin. We shall see now what happens. Don't fail me, Britt, or we are sunk. . . .

Actually, more detailed inspection later in the day revealed that in my joy in dumping Archie's grub overboard, I had been carried away, and my supplies were not likely to last for more than twenty days. Up till then I had been using mostly canned stuff, foraged from the ships we had met along the way. The cans I had simply distributed, more or less evenly, in all eight watertight compartments, dipping in whenever I felt the urge to treat myself to a delicacy.

Whether I had been indulging my particular fancies more often than I thought, or whether the number of tins had been less than I figured, the fact was that I had miscalculated. Not that it would make much difference. With the few pounds of rice I had left over from the *Skauborg* I intended to make a fish stew every other day, thereby hoping to postpone to a considerable extent the time when I would have to rely on fish alone.

The main hardship was going to be fitting two extra hours into my daily ten-hour rowing schedule, as doing with less than five hours' sleep was out of the question. After careful consideration, this is how I decided to go about it: wake up at five in the morning, row ninety minutes, ten-minute break, row ninety minutes, rest for one hour. Breakfast, cigarette, odd things. Again, row ninety minutes, ten-minute break, row ninety minutes. By then it would be roughly twelve-thirty. I could then try to take things as easy as possible until five in the afternoon, then start rowing again and continue, keeping the same routine as in the morning, until midnight, when I could go to sleep, and so on. In practice, I knew that I could hardly expect to be able to keep to such a tight schedule every day, as the few hours left free to do the thousand and one chores demanded by everyday life on *Britannia*, such as cooking, fishing, writing the Log, navigating, distilling water, calling London by radio once a week (after which I had to start the generator to recharge the batteries) and filming for ITN, not to mention keeping *Britannia* shipshape, were bound to prove insufficient. Suffice it to say that I had two books with me, paperback novels. One had gone overboard, unopened. The other, *Where Eagles Dare,* by Alistair MacLean, I had read as far as Chapter 3. So now, perhaps, when he sees, at the end of a Log entry, "Rowed twelve hours," the reader will have a better understanding of what the day had been like and how I felt. And if it says less than twelve hours or, for that matter, none at all, may I expect to be forgiven for breaking my self-imposed discipline?

Mar. 26   65th day
Magnificent! Wind from the east, increasing to Force 6. Keep blowing, God damn it!
Rowed twelve hours. Tired, wet, but in fine spirits.

Mar. 27   66th day
Wind from the east, Force 6–7.
Can't believe it, but there it is! Britannia is wonderful; we fly!
Rowed twelve hours. Too tired to write.

Mar. 28   67th day
Same. Wind from the east, Force 6–7.
Having a horrible time; everything wet. Wave crests break-ing in every so often, as Britannia gets broadside when I lose control or when I am not rowing, since I then let her drift without the drogue. Tons of water at a time. But she is mag-nificent; her self-bailing system works perfectly. Dry again in about one minute from being completely swamped (water up to gunwales). All is wet, but watertight compartments seem to be O.K. Can't open to check yet.
Rowed ten hours.

Mar. 29   68th day
Easing up a bit. Wind from the east, Force 6.
Still shipping water; waves ten, fifteen feet high. Having a miserable time.
Rowed twelve hours.

Mar. 30   69th day
Same as yesterday.
Rowed ten hours.

Mar. 31   70th day
Same.
Rowed twelve hours.

Rough weather at sea.

Sunset at sea after a calm day.

Strong winds from the east. Incredible! Marvelous! Of course, had they been from the southeast it would have been better still, as then we would have recovered some latitude as well; but let us not tempt the gods by being too greedy.

As it was, I could not have hoped for a greater boost to my morale, and I felt elated. Nevertheless, what was good to the spirit was misery to the flesh. Weathering a near gale in an open boat with practically no freeboard was sheer hell—worse than living in a bathtub, as things, and myself, could not then have been reduced more thoroughly to a state of permanent immersion. Whether I manned the oars or crept into my rathole made absolutely no difference. All the rathole could do, and this to a limited extent, was keep the wind off my back. The sea knew no such limitations. Without the drogue to keep her head-on to the waves (with an easterly wind, checking *Britannia's* drift was clearly out of the question), an average of one out of fifty-five—I took the trouble of counting them—would break over the side in a deluge of foam. In a second *Britannia* would be swamped, the water up to the gunwales, and if I happened to be lying inside the rathole I would find myself actually floating, nose bumping against the Plastazote top. This did not in the least impair *Britannia's* seaworthiness, as, unlike normal boats, she had been designed with precisely this in mind. The assurance that, as long as the hatch covers leading to the eight compartments belowdecks kept a watertight seal, *Britannia* would always float like a cork, and the fact that I was spared the backbreaking task of bailing, were a great help, and I bow with humble respect to Uffa's genius.

Sadly, an open rowboat is an open rowboat, and while I hoped that everything that mattered—generator, batteries, radio—would remain dry, the one thing I could not do was cook. By the same token, I could not distill seawater, and my emergency reserve of two gallons had dwindled to precious little. For this reason, wishing to keep my water consumption to a minimum, I ate next to nothing. I wasn't particularly hungry anyway, but as a result of skimping on food, I felt cold, frozen, right to the marrow. Damn weather; how long was it going to last?

"Venus, my beloved, I did ask you to send some strong, easterly winds, but don't you think you are overdoing it? Can't you ease up a little? Too much of a good thing can kill one just the same as anything else."

I was dying for a cup of boiling-hot tea!

Apr. 1   *71st day*
Wind dropped during the night; Force 3–4, still from the east. Position at dusk 18°40′ North, 31°00′ West.
I feel now completely justified in jettisoning all that stuff. It was a gamble, but my judgment proved sound, and with a bit of luck windwise, I think we'll make it. The important thing now is to keep our latitude and, if possible—with an easterly wind it should be—recover some. I would like to cross the shipping lane at, more or less, 20°00′ North, 40°00′ West. Perhaps it's too much to ask, but I will try my God-damnedest. I have food for about eighteen days. Will have to be very accurate in my navigation, because if I pass the shipping lane without knowing—and it can't be more than a few miles wide—there will be no turning back, and the next shipping lane is a good six hundred miles farther west. The thought of missing out and eating nothing but fish for six hundred miles makes me shudder. I have never liked fish so very much anyway. We shall see.
Rowed twelve hours.

I had jolly good reasons to be happy. In the last nine days we had covered three hundred miles with a loss of only thirty miles of latitude, an average of thirty-three miles per day. Four hundred pounds lighter and riding about an inch higher in the water, *Britannia* had handled herself with much greater ease, and the effort required by rowing seemed to have decreased out of all proportion to the weight unloaded. I could not expect the easterlies to blow forever at Force 6—indeed, I had absolutely no wish for that—but if they held for a week or so at about Force 3–4, I could expect to recover one or two degrees of latitude and, maybe, keep the same average, if not actually increase it. A Force-4 (eleven to sixteen knots) wind was ideal from the rowing point of view. Anything stronger than that increased the difficulties of steering *Britannia* on a straight course to the detriment of speed—so much so that, provided it came from the right quarter, I would rather have too little than too much wind.

During these last days I had not been able to feed Jerrycan and the boys, but it was heartwarming to see that they were still around. Lately, we had also acquired an escort of a dozen or so pilot fish—most of them survivors of the hammerhead, clearly at a loss as to where to go after their master's departure. The dolphins were not in the least impressed with their possibilities as appetizers—and to be honest, neither was I, since a pilot fish's diet is based on shark excreta.

By boiling seawater almost nonstop for fifteen hours, I had managed to distill a gallon and a half, and hoped to start doing the same the first thing on the morrow.

For dinner I had my special Sunday stew: a tin of corned beef, one of mixed vegetables, one of tomato soup and plenty of spices; mix well, stir, bring to the boil, eat. Fifteen minutes in all. For its simplicity and tastiness, this particular concoction has always been one of my favorites—constituting, together with eggs scrambled with spinach, my own staple bachelor diet during hard times ashore with no money or girls to look after me.

Apr. 2   *72nd day*
Wind still from the east, Force 4–5, but the sky—it is now 1300 GMT—is getting very dark. Massive formations of low clouds gathering to the east. Looks as if my wanton goddess is finally becoming awake to my needs. Hope she remembers

I am but a simple mortal and, in trying to make up for her past inattentions, doesn't smother me in a sudden burst of solicitude. However much I love her, I am not sure that I like the idea of giving my all in her Olympian arms—not at my tender age, anyway. Maybe it will only be a passing squall. 2400 GMT. Passing squall, my foot—it's a bloody gale! Force 6–7, gusting to 8; rain; waves fifteen, twenty feet high. Lost one drogue. Cannot write any more, too much rolling. . . .

What had seemed in the early afternoon to be no more than a bit of rough weather gained force into the night until it became so bad that I had attempted, while not rowing, to stream a drogue in an effort to prevent the nearly continuous swamping of *Britannia*; but the flimsy thing—made not of canvas, but of light nylon—had proved too small to withstand the strain of holding *Britannia* in gale-force winds, and was torn to pieces in only half an hour. Luckily, soon afterward the clouds' waterlogged bowels discharged in a blinding downpour. Heavy rain has a soothing, mollifying effect on wild seas, comparable to that of an oil slick.

Apr. 3, 4 and 5   73rd, 74th and 75th days
Still going like hell; easterly winds, Force 7–8, gusting 9. All wet, shipping water all the time. Hope radio and generator are O.K. Never had it so bad before. Rowing in diving suit. Cannot sleep because lost another drogue and remaining one shredded to bits. Using bucket as drogue, but not very effective—must man the oars continuously to keep Britannia from broaching. Very tired, almost dead from want of rest and wish to hell . . . Shit-all! Nearly capsized this time. Will write again when weather improves.

Seen from *Britannia's* level—that is, below water—the difference between a full gale and a hurricane existed in name only. For four days we rode the backs of rampaging white horses, playing a game of toss-and-tumble with them.

It was a very simple game, with no particular set of rules. All that was required of the rider was to try and hang on as long as possible, while he could be tossed and tumbled at will and, whenever the opportunity presented itself, kicked about from all angles. He was not allowed to protest, retaliate or hope to win—just hang on and take it.

To prevent myself from being swept overboard, I had two lines attached at all times to my harness—one lashed to port, the other to starboard. I kept them extremely short so that in the unlikely event of a capsize, I could be confident of remaining on board. That way, if I bashed myself into unconsciousness, I could be sure of not drowning—safe in the knowledge that *Britannia* would right herself in two seconds flat. This reduced my movements to a minimum, but there was nowhere to go. When I was not sitting on the sliding seat, straining to keep head-on to the wind, I was lying inside the rathole.

To give an accurate description of the misery of those four days is quite beyond my pen. And in any case, after two days of continuous, relentless punishment, I became a doddering idiot. The rest of the gale I spent in a daze, my actions being those of a well-trained zombie. The last day I spent mostly in the rathole—half lying on deck, half floating on it. I slept, dreamed I was drowning and went on sleeping. Whatever happened, I would not have given a damn. . . .

Apr. 6   *76th day*
Wind from the east, Force 4–5. Heavy swell.
Every now and then a wave crest still gets in; all the same, it is much better now. It is completely overcast and I cannot take my position. Wonder where the hell we are now? Must have made pretty good speed. During the gale I rowed much less, in fact hardly rowed at all in the strict sense, but had to man the oars most of the time to keep Britannia *from broaching. It was terribly exhausting as, inevitably, I had to pull more on one side than on the other and really pull—that is,*

*use all my strength—just to keep her straight. However,
there were times when we seemed to be flying, and I am
very hopeful to have made good progress.*
Rowed only ten hours today to catch back my breath a bit.

Apr. 7   77th day
Wind from the east, Force 5.
*Still overcast, but not so much; maybe it will clear later. Very
happy about the wind: as long as it stays easterly, everything
will be fine. Life has been very rough lately, but if I have kept
my latitude and made good progress, it will have been worth
my pains. If I could only take a day or two to rest . . . But
I can't afford it, as it would mean, most certainly, loss of
latitude and make everything a lot worse later on. Florida is
so far away still, but Venus is helping me. She came to me last
night, resplendent in her naked beauty. She promised me that
as long as I keep fighting, I would get to Florida, and even
predicted a date—June 27. I write it down at this stage, when
everything is so uncertain that I could not even predict the
month, let alone the date, of my arrival, so as not to forget.
She predicted something for me years ago, only I didn't believe it, and when it came true I could have shot myself for
a fool.*
Rowed twelve hours.

Apr. 8   78th day
Wind still from the east, Force 4–5.
*This is very good indeed, but raining continuously and rather
cold. Not too bad for rowing, though. At dawn our position
was extraordinarily good: 19°00′ North, 35°30′ West. So we
have kept our latitude—even gained a bit; and this is fantastic, as it is the first time we have been able to do so. Shows
what a difference an easterly wind can make.*

I could not altogether rely on the accuracy of this position,
because I had barely managed to get two very quick shots,
through a hole in the clouds, of Arcturus and the planet

Mars. In fact, I was probably a bit off—as, in my haste, chances were I had miscalculated the altitude of one, if not both, stars. Without a third position line it was impossible to judge how big this error might be, but I knew by instinct it was within reason. This being so, in the last seven days we had covered a distance of two hundred and seventy miles, an average of roughly thirty-eight miles per day—and in the process, recovered twenty miles of latitude. Such progress went beyond my wildest hopes, and I became very confident that from then on, an average of thirty miles per day was well within my capability—as long, that is, as the easterlies held.

My boys are still with us—they have been since March 15— and I keep them happy by feeding them scraps of the unfortunate victims of my spear. I know they are the same ones, as, besides Jerrycan, they all have scars now where I have marked them with my knife—they come so near when I feed them, it's easy—so as to be able to recognize them and see how far they will come with us. Also, it saves their lives: new ones are constantly joining them, and I never shoot the ones with my brand. They are the only fish I have seen so far, almost, aside from sharks and flying ones. I am still waiting to see a porpoise, but no luck. Anyway, my boys got into a school of flying fish this morning, so near to Britannia that they flew into her. Plenty of them struck Britannia, and one struck me—rather painfully, too. Five fell in, so I had a delicious breakfast. Beginning to feel less tired now, and twelve hours' rowing seems to be O.K. My major complaint is boredom.
Rowed twelve hours.

Apr. 9   *79th day*
Wind from the east, Force 4–5.
Still raining occasionally. It's been a quiet day; nothing happened. Bored.
Rowed twelve hours.

Bored? How can one feel boredom without a single minute to spare, without a chance to spend a single hour lazing? Yet bored I was.

My ennui stemmed not from lack of occupation but from the monotony of doing the same things over and over again. Even my distractions—catching a shark or watching the antics of my boys—were beginning to lose their interest. Furthermore, weathering the gale had seemingly left a void in my mind. Gradually but inexorably, the ceaseless struggle for survival, coupled with the backbreaking, soul-destroying task of manning the oars for hours on end, was subduing my vital energy. In order to survive I was returning to the primeval, shedding the veneer with which civilization had coated my animal instincts. I became a naked savage, a beast of prey that to feel alive was compelled to search for means of escaping the tediousness that threatened to smother the urge to go on fighting. Because I was almost always desperately tired, every now and then I had to find release from my self-imposed slavery. Somehow I could still laugh at myself—that, and bloody, reckless sorties against the fish that *Britannia* lured to her, were my best outlets.

Apr. 10   *80th day*
Wind from the east, Forces 4–5, and sunshine. About time, as my tan was beginning to fade.
A new dolphin arrived today, so terribly mauled that he could hardly swim, so I put him out of his misery and fed him to the others. As I did so, I noticed a stranger partaking in the feast. Should have said in the odors of the feast, as nobody seems to be fast enough to take anything off my boys. About six feet long and at least a hundred pounds in weight, the newcomer was of a species unknown to me; but I could not resist the temptation of a bit of action, and tying a safety line round my waist, I went overboard with the spear gun, asking for trouble.
The stranger came straight at me and circled around, un-

*doubtedly flabbergasted at the sight of such a funny fish. I
have had plenty of scraps with big ones, but by the gods, I
would be hard put to remember, offhand, one that ever gave
me a better fight. In spite of my getting in a near-perfect shot,
it took me fifteen minutes before I could get near enough to
rip his belly with my knife—a necessary operation, as otherwise I would never have been able to take him on board. By
this time the aquamarine of the sea around us was tinged
with blood, and the boys were swimming frenziedly about.
You can imagine the sight—they are nearly a hundred by
now! Soon, as the entrails of the "big one" hung out, they
struck at him, and as I was holding him by the spear shaft,
they flashed by, inches away from my face and body, sometimes actually brushing me aside—and, golly! they are quite
big too. I was at the end of my safety line, some twenty yards
from* Britannia, *and I began to get worried about what would
happen if they decided to attack me. Anyway, sharks were
bound to arrive at any moment now, and I had to get the
brute on* Britannia—*or what was left of him.*

*I had never guessed twenty yards could be so long. The "big
one" was not dead yet. As if that were not enough, every time
a dolphin took a bite off him it also gave a tremendous pull,
which stopped my progress toward* Britannia *and pulled me
back to the end of my lifeline. Five minutes afterward, a
third of the "big one" gone, I was still at the end of the line,
unable to make any progress. Eventually I managed to join
the line of the spear gun to my lifeline and, by pulling myself
along the latter, climbed back on board. I then retrieved my
prize the same way. The spear was bent out of recognition,
and so was the "big one." Furthermore, I was covered with
blood—which, to my amazement, I discovered was my own.
I had scratches all over, some of them quite big scratches,
undoubtedly made by the dolphins as they swished by. In
the frenzy of battle I just hadn't noticed. I do now—they
burn like hell! My hands are somewhat damaged too. All in
all, I feel a lot more bruised than after my scrap with the*

mako; but by Jupiter, such is the sport of kings—and as I re-
live it now, I can feel my blood run hot again.
The sharks arrived, too late. But not for me—I killed two,
and my boys had never eaten so much in their lives.
Rowed only seven hours. What the hell, must get some joy
out of this caper every now and then.

Apr. 11   *81st day*
Wind from the east, Force 4–5.
This is great. If this turnabout of my luck holds, I shall be doing fine. But I don't feel fine at all, and the last thing I want
to do today is row. First of all, I feel so bruised and battered,
as if a steamroller had gone over me; and then that big brute
of a fish has avenged himself in a most fiendish way. As I
mentioned before, I never had seen one like it, and I decided
to find out what it tasted like. The meat seemed white and
juicy, much better-looking than that of my dolphins. So, having run out of cayenne pepper, I decided to open a little
bottle of Tabasco sauce I kept for occasions such as this.
Well, I figured only a few drops at a time would come out of
it and shook the bottle vigorously. When I stopped, I discovered, to my horror, that nearly half of my precious treasure
had gone into just a pound of fish and a fistful of rice. I was
so hungry I ate it all, but for the life of me, I couldn't say
what that fish tasted like. The trouble is, my stomach didn't
seem to appreciate it and is now working overtime trying to
get rid of it. I can just imagine, as I squat over the gunwale,
what that big fish must be thinking as he looks up from the
bottom, or wherever dead fish go: Well, well! Look at that,
now. Ain't that bastard that went and done for me made a
big ass of himself? What a laugh!
Don't feel like rowing at all, yet row I must. Ten hours today.
What a big ass indeed!

9

Apr. 12   82nd day

Wind dropped today: Force 3–4 only; but still from the east.
This is indeed very, very good. It allows me not only to keep
my latitude but also to regain some. If it goes on like this, I
am hoping to reach the shipping lane in five to six days' time,
and to do so at roughly 20° North Latitude, 40° West Longitude—and this is a hell of a lot better than my wildest dreams
of twenty days ago. The beauty of it is that according to the
American Pilot Chart for April, the farther west we go the
more easterly winds we should have. I just hope they are
right. Florida, wait for us—we are coming!

Rowed twelve hours.

Apr. 13   83rd day

Venus—my adorable, beautiful, gorgeous Venus—you are the

greatest! Keep pushing for me, keep pushing, and we'll make it.
Winds still from the east, Force 3–4.
Position at sunset 19° 32′ North, 38° 00′ West.
Unbelievable the amount of latitude we have gained: thirty miles in five days, no less. Never been so happy in my life. Keep rowing, Britannia. Keep rowing, God damn it all, and we'll make it, by the gods!
Rowed thirteen hours today to celebrate. Am dead.

There were many reasons for my happiness. *Britannia's* behavior and her increased speed were proof that my judgment in throwing overboard most of the stores had been sound. That was a tremendous satisfaction to me, since my shore-based friends had regarded my action as little short of lunacy, the act of a mind deranged by fatigue and privation.

Admittedly, from a dispassionate, commonsense outlook, it had been all that and probably more. Until then, as far as survival was concerned, I had been entirely self-sufficient, whereas now I was entirely dependent on fish and passing ships. My ability to catch fish was unquestionable provided there were any to be caught. As for ships, shipping lanes or no shipping lanes, I had no guarantee whatsoever of seeing any, let alone of being sighted. The wind could change as well; most likely it would. What then? These were the imponderables, and I had willingly put myself at their mercy.

At the moment my goal was to reach Florida, to conquer the Atlantic as I had set my mind to, and everything, absolutely everything, had to be subservient to that ambition. This was an obsession, something I *had* to do—or perish. What price I would have to pay, how hard I would have to fight still and what temptations I would have to resist, I did not know, would not know, until the very last day, when I would set foot on the golden beaches of Florida. To achieve this I was determined to pit myself against all the odds, to push my luck to the very limit and, if necessary, beyond that limit, whatever it might be. For the moment, my gamble was paying off, and I was happy, deliriously happy. Oh, I knew it would not last. My happiness was like a fragile, iridescent bubble, as delicate as it was beautiful, bound to burst at the least pinprick; but not yet, not until tomorrow. . . . And what's tomorrow compared with the present?

Apr. 14   *84th day*

Wind still from the east, very light—Force 2–3.
Since yesterday I have started to row due north, taking advantage of the easterly winds and the relative calm of the sea. This is ideal weather in which to try and regain some latitude, and I intend to do so, even at the sacrifice of a bit of longitude. However, wind and current should make us drift toward the west; this, abetted by the time during which I am not rowing, should keep us going west without, I hope, preventing us from gaining latitude at a much faster rate than before. Rowing north, it will take me longer to reach the shipping lane—probably three or four days more, always provided this weather holds. But I am not worried, although I have run out of pipe tobacco, and my food will last only four more days. After that it will have to be fish every day until we meet a ship—on April 20–21, with luck. If I miss sighting a ship there will be, of course, no turning back, and I will have to push on until the next shipping lane—about fifteen to twenty days' rowing time (that is to say, twenty days from the moment we reach Longitude 40°). The prospect of eating nothing but fish for all that time makes me shudder, but I am prepared to accept it. Have vitamin pills and glucose powder to make a balanced diet, and it should see me through in a fit condition.
Rowed twelve hours.

Apr. 15   *85th day,*

Wind same, and at sunset our position was 20°32′ North,

38°35′ West. A gain of one degree of latitude in two days.
Wonderful! Feel very tired but still happy.
Rowed twelve hours.

Apr. 16   *86th day*
Easterly winds, Force 4.
Rowing northwest again, ten hours only—needed a little bit of rest.

Apr. 17   *87th day*
Wind from the east, Force 4.
Dorados still with us, tirelessly prancing about. I have food for only one more day—after which, unless I stop a ship, it will be fish forever. Smoked my last cigar, too, and have tobacco for two pipes only, and the tobacco is not even pipe tobacco but cigar butts. I am not really sure which bothers me more: eating fish, or not smoking. And to think that I wanted to quit smoking during this trip!
Rowed twelve hours.

The weather was absolutely marvelous. Under a cloudless, sunny sky, the sea, gently combed by the wind, was an undulating prairie of deep, undiluted blue, with a scattering of isolated, idly roaming white horses. With waves seldom exceeding five feet in height, life in *Britannia* was not only pleasant but, compared with what it had been, almost luxurious. If only I did not have to row! But row I had to. As the days went by, to complete my twelve-hour schedule required just that little bit of extra effort, and at the end of it, I felt just that little bit more fatigued than the previous day. How long before the flesh would refuse to obey the commands of the mind? How long before the spirit would cease to supply the mind with the energy to give orders?

Beautiful days, yes. But would there be a day in my life, would I ever again live to see dawn, without having to face the grueling prospect of rowing, rowing, rowing, nothing but rowing? I wondered.

Apr. 18   *88th day*
Winds from the east, Force 4–5. Overcast. Squally.
Sighted a ship in the midst of a squall, late afternoon, right on my bows, but too far away to call their attention. Am not yet really in the shipping lane proper, so this must have been an errant one. Our position is 21°09′ North, 40°10′ West. Feeling slightly overtired, but otherwise O.K. What I resent most is the sheer boredom of it. Am beginning to feel like an animal, a rowing machine, not a human being any longer. At the beginning I used to sing while rowing, until I got hoarse, but eventually I could not bring myself to sing anymore. Tried hard then, as I rowed, to think of something serious or important to me; but even that seems impossible now. I start thinking, but I finish by staring blankly at some distant point during the day, or at a star at night. I go on rowing automatically, without even noticing what I am doing. What a hell of a way to live!
Rowed twelve hours.

The New York–Cape of Good Hope shipping lane ran at a tangent to my own course, and because of this, now that I had recovered so much latitude, our paths would cross a bit farther west than would have been the case had I remained south of Latitude 20°.

Naturally, a ship does not follow a shipping lane in the same way in which a car follows a road—a shipping lane being an imaginary line along, when great distances are involved, a Great Circle course: that is, the shortest route between a ship's ports of departure and destination. Nevertheless, since distance and time are equated in terms of hard cash, a merchant ship's captain, unless otherwise compelled by navigational hazards, will always take his ship from A to

B along the same course, internationally agreed on and shown on the Pilot Charts as North Atlantic Lane routes. Anywhere in their vicinity I could expect to see a ship. As I had done so within two days of my estimate, it meant that my navigation was spot on, and this, of course, pleased me. The *Talsy*, way back on February 24, had been my last ship, and seeing one after so long, even if we had not been spotted, was just as cheering.

Unless one has been for a considerable time alone at sea in a small boat, it is impossible to appreciate the absolute limitlessness of it all. How unimaginable it feels to sleep and wake, each time, with the knowledge that one is floating in a blue void, suspended between a fathomless abyss and infinite space, without a single tangible landmark to give an idea of speed or progress, or even a wake to prove one is moving. There is nothing other than a few impersonal dots and numbers jotted down on a sheet of paper. Yesterday we were there; today we are here; tomorrow, perhaps, there. All very neat and logical, but emotionally without reality—and for a lonely rower, struggling in a world of watery nothingness in his lonely boat, realities were all-important.

Apr. 19   *89th day*
Wind from the east, Force 4–5. Overcast but no rain.
Sylvia was on the radio today and this has cheered me up a bit, but I hardly know what to talk about with her any more. I am getting stupid, there is no doubt about it. My reflexes have slowed, and when spear fishing I miss shots I would never have missed before; and my judgment of distance and refraction has gone to hell.
Still two and a half months to go! Have never sailed in my life, but the way I see it, sailing, whether single-handed or not, is just a joke, a childish game, compared with rowing. Today has been a really terrible one. Nothing whatever went right. Nearly lost Britannia, *then cut my hand on the palm, and it hurts like hell when rowing. Lost a spear. The burner*

Self-portrait of J. F., taken at sea.

Huge hammerhead shark, lassoed and held to the side of the boat.

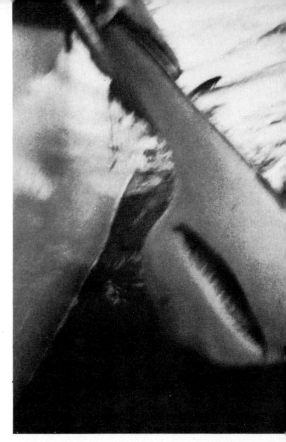

J. F. poses for a self-portrait at sea with the desiccated head of the hammerhead shark, kept as a trophy.

broke and had to be replaced, and I smoked my last pipe,
God damn it! And ate fish for breakfast, lunch and dinner.
Oh, I have had enough. Good night!
Rowed eleven hours.

Lately my moods had tended to go up and down like a yo-
yo. The slightest accidents or events, things that normally I
would have accepted with a smile or dismissed with a shrug,
were beginning to influence my temper in utter irrelevance
to cause and effect.

To see Jerrycan, big mouth wide open, go all out after a
tasty bit, only to have it snatched away at the very last moment by a faster, and usually much smaller, brother was
enough to have me roaring with hilarity. An hour later, an
untimely shower of spray would reduce me to unbelievable
extremes of madness, and during such periods, in my hate
against the sea, I was capable of almost anything—such as
shooting at the crest of an oncoming wave, which is how I
lost a spear. And some days could be absolute murder
throughout.

Take today, which I had started by catching a dorado. A
monstrous newcomer I had speared for the sole reason that it
was so big. I usually chose smaller ones, much easier to
handle, but this time I had not been able to resist the temptation. After spearing him through the body (as lousy a shot as
there could be), I had finally managed to haul him on board
—where he went berserk. Gushing blood in torrents, spilling
his innards all over the deck, the wildly thrashing brute
threatened to wreck everything in sight unless I managed to
hold him, which I attempted to do by throwing myself with
all my weight on top of him.

Has anyone ever tried to hold still, by the sheer force of his
bare hands and legs—and this on the cramped, bobbing deck
of a rowboat—a slippery, steely-muscled, fighting-mad, five-
foot, fifty-pound dorado? One minute I was on top; the next
he struck such a terrific tail blow between my legs, hitting

the inside of my thigh and grazing my groin, that I shot up-
right in a spasm of searing pain. Immediately my legs turned
to rubber, and I bent sideways and toppled overboard with
the grace of a sack of potatoes. As I came up again, *Britannia*
came down, and Bang!—something in my head exploded in a
multicolored display of fireworks.

The traitorous bitch!

Stunned into semiconsciousness, swallowing water, desperately coughing and gasping for air, I failed to grab hold
of the gunwale, and *Britannia*, bent on mutiny, pandemonium still rampant on her decks, slowly drifted away. I saw
her go through dazed, tear-filled eyes, utterly incapable of
pulling a single stroke in her pursuit. The pain in my groin
held me paralyzed; I could only float, concentrating franti-
cally upon the overriding, vital need to keep my head above
water.

Britannia's self-bailing deck had been designed to lie three
inches above her waterline. Thus, when I was standing on
deck, the gunwales would come only to the height of my
calves. Since her beam amidships was only four feet nine
inches, it had been clear from the beginning that the danger
of my parting company with *Britannia* would be ever-
present, either by the boat's tipping or by my being washed
overboard, making it imperative to keep a safety line permanently attached to my waist.

This I had always done—during the first fortnight or so.
After that, the nuisance of having the line forever tangling
onto something every time I moved became too great to
bear. In any case, I had developed, and felt exceedingly
cocky about, a surefooted, fine sense of balance. Finally I
had dispensed with the safety line, in practically all weather
less than a near gale.

All the same, just in case, I usually had a sixty-foot nylon
warp trailing after *Britannia*. It was this warp that I managed to grab as it sneaked past me, and hanging on for dear
life, I let *Britannia* tow me for a while. Eventually, feeling

wobbly and a bit nauseated still, I managed to pull myself back on board.

The dolphin had thrashed his way into the rathole, effectively forfeiting whatever chances he might have had of heaving himself over the side; but the mess was appalling. Wearily dragging the fast-stiffening carcass into the open, I damned all fish to fry in hell forevermore. It took me nearly two hours to tidy up and put matters right. Then, while gutting him, I cut my hand. A clean, deep, dastardly painful cut, right on the palm where it would hurt most when I was rowing.

Nor was that all: as the blasted burner chose that particular day to go bust! Luckily, I had a spare—considering my total helplessness with all things mechanical.

Smoking what I knew to be my last pipe at the end of the day was the last straw. As I wrote: for one day, I had had enough!

Apr. 20   *90th day*
Wind from the east, Force 4–5.
Well, I am supposed to be in the shipping lane—where are the ships? Not around here, that's for sure. It's a bit too soon to say yet, but I don't like the looks of it. Off the Canary Islands it was like Piccadilly Circus, so much so that I lived in fear of being run down. I didn't really need ships then. Now I do and they are not around.
Thought for the day: I hate fish! And today, without even a fag, I am celebrating three months since departure.
Rowed twelve hours.

Apr. 21   *91st day*
Wind from the east, Force 4–5.
In this wind I cannot hope to stay around for long, and I am not even trying. Either we meet a ship or we don't. At our speed we should give them more than enough time to come around, even if the lane is not a very busy one, but no luck

today. Saw two ships, but so far away it was out of the ques-
tion to try and attract their attention. I feel sad, despondent
and very bad-tempered. My hand hurts like hell and it's a bit
swollen, but I must go on rowing. Oh, Florida, you'd better
be beautiful and nice to me when I get there because you are
really costing me dear!
Rowed eleven hours.

Apr. 22   92nd day
Wind from the east, Force 3–4.
Fine day for meeting a ship, but to hell with them—none
came. I must go on. Have vitamin pills for one hundred days.
One pound of rice. Plenty of pepper and spices. That's all.
Rowed twelve hours.

That day my mood was so rotten, I nearly murdered Jerrycan.

I was washing my wounded hand over the side when he
whooshed out of nowhere and snapped at it, missing by an
inch. Honestly, after all I had done for the bugger: saving
the juiciest, tastiest bits of everything for him; treating him
like my only, very best friend! And what did I get for it? The
first time, the day he bit my finger, it could have been a mistake. After all, I was washing a spoon and he might, just
might, have mistaken its silvery gleam for that of a fish. Now
he had no excuse.

"Jerrycan, you damn well knew it was my hand. My poor,
battered, swollen, bleeding little hand, and you went for it,
like a greedy, shameless, ungrateful swine. What will you try
to bite next? My . . . ? Damn it all, you asked for it!"

With the spear gun cocked and ready, finger hovering on
the trigger, I waited for Jerrycan to approach, trailing the
point of the spear underwater. And what happened? The unspeakable so-and-so came up to it, gave the spear a nudge
and tried to bite it!

"God damn you, Jerrycan, how stupid can you get? Don't

you realize what it means? All I have to do is press my finger a fraction of an inch and it will be death you swallow!"

Jerrycan turned sideways, peering at me questioningly with the dumbest expression I had ever seen, or could ever hope to see, on a fish. "So help me, Jerrycan, if I'm not—" But I just couldn't bring myself to kill him. Disgraceful beggar got away with it!

Apr. 23   *93rd day*
Wind from the east, Force 3–4.
Position yesterday at sunset was 20°55′ North, 42°30′ West.
We seem to be doing very well. St. George's Day. Heard on the radio, World Service of the BBC, that Knox-Johnston has made it. Good for him! Asked Sylvia to send him a cable from me for a well-done job. What really gets me is that, apparently, he called his journey a pleasant holiday. How I wish I could say the same!
Rowed twelve hours.

Aside from the Marconi, I had a transistor radio, which I used mainly to keep an eye on the doings of what passed as my ship's chronometer: wristwatch—Rolex GMT-Master. I must say that as watches go, the Rolex was damned good, gaining only two seconds per day and never varying the rate, which is all that matters in a chronometer. All the same, I checked every day by tuning in to the BBC World Service at 1800 hours GMT. That was generally all, and only occasionally did I go on listening to the news. It may seem strange, but I loathed having my solitude shattered by the sound of human voices chattering on matters and events happening so far away from my present world that I had lost all possible interest in them. All I craved, and even this only now and then, was a good concert. To listen to Beethoven's Fifth or Ninth symphony, for instance, would have been marvelous. Unfortunately, all the world seemed to be interested in listening to was bloody pop music, and rather than defile the

natural melodies of seas and winds with that, I would have
thrown the transistor over the side.

Apr. 24   *94th day*
Wind from the east, Force 2–3. Overcast.
A ship passed by at no more than three miles at 0800 local
time, and did not see us—unbelievable but true. I sent my
oilskin on top of the aerial to a height of about twenty feet,
to no avail. Fired three smoke signals, the last one on top of
the aerial, and the orange smoke went up in a cloud in rela-
tively still air—yet they sailed majestically on, so near I could
see their waterline.
How about that? I know now, or at least can pretty well
guess, what it must be like for a real castaway in the last
stages of exhaustion to see a ship pass him by. I don't really
need a ship badly. I can make my own drinking water, as
long as the Ronson lasts anyway, and fish my own food. A
bit of an exercise in survival at sea now—uncomfortable, but
nothing else, yet. Still, I would very much like a bit of to-
bacco and some decent grub. I miss more than anything else
the relaxing pipe I used to smoke at the end of a hard day.
Life out here is miserable enough without unnecessary added
hardships, so I feel pretty cheesed off about it. This must have
been another stray out of the lane proper, but maybe Venus
will help a bit. We'll see. No, nothing doing.
Rowed twelve hours.

The primary duty of the Officer of the Watch is to see that,
at all times, a proper lookout is kept. This is the rule, without
exception, for any and all ships. However, in this day and age
of automatic pilots and whatnot, it is not at all uncommon
for the bridge to be left under the care of a single man,
sometimes not even an officer, and if the ship in question is
happily plodding her way on the high seas, on a clear day,
human nature being what it is . . .

Apr. 25   *95th day*
Wind from the east, Force 3–4.
*Come to think of it, I am very grateful about the weather.
Since April 1 we have had nothing but easterly winds. I do
hope my luck holds. At sunset I spotted another ship, but this
one was too far. I can see them but they can't see us. The fate
of the castaway must be a very sorry one. I miss, most of all,
my pipe. I think I have said this before, but it was, in a way
still is, my best companion. It is a funny thing, but I usually
don't bother much about smoking a pipe when life is normal.
Then cigarettes will do just as well, or better; but as soon as
I find myself in an adventure, be it hunting in some remote
South American bush or on the seas, I have always found my
pipe the best of friends.
Ate a lot of fish today. Don't like it, but ye gods, I'm hungry!
The dolphins are still with us, more beautiful than ever, and
the water being so clear, it is great entertainment to watch
their antics. They like to swim sideways under* Britannia, *and
on nights of full moon, or even half moon, as now, they shine
in such an incredible display of silvery spots that we seem
at times to be floating over a chestful of liquid silver. I have
had opportunities to curse them often when I had to go on
rowing past my sleeping hour, just because I had lost time in
their contemplation. Today, by the way, I ate barracuda.
Two of the fish paid us a visit (first time), and one of them
stayed.
Rowed eleven hours.*

*Same day, 0300 local time.
Did I say that I have changed my working hours from GMT
to zone time? No matter.
For some reason or other I cannot sleep tonight. I am tired—
so tired that I did not row twelve hours, but eleven—and yet
I cannot sleep. It is strange, because it has never happened
before. It's very calm, the wind a bare whisper; the moon is*

half full—and I cannot sleep. With eyes open I lay down, looking at the ceiling of my rathole, thinking that it looked exactly like the inside of a coffin. A deluxe one at that. So in the end I got up and out, and am now writing, but I do not feel like writing. It is a pity I don't have a tape recorder. To-night I want to think and, in a way, dream. Writing simply spoils everything; it's like having company. I have been so many days alone, but I want to be alone tonight—just the sea and myself. Somehow, I wish the dawn would never come. I shall be very sad at dawn. Don't know why.

Apr. 26   *96th day*
Wind from the east, Force 3–4.
Nice morning and "everything's going my way." Wish I could sing properly. Haven't slept at all, and to say that I'm worn out would be an understatement. Oh, Florida, you are going to take years out of my life! But I am gaining latitude all the time, and as long as the easterlies continue to blow I shall keep doing so. If I can only manage to stay above Lati-tude 20 I shall get some southeasterlies too, during May—I am sure I will. May is my month. I was born in May—the twenty-first, to be precise. It will be a lonely birthday this year. Will I still be around by then? What a silly thought. Of course I will. But I won't be alone. Me and the dolphins and the sea. And Britannia.
Rowed twelve hours.

I was getting sentimental. And soft, in the head as well as everywhere else. I cried out to my precious Venus: "You have sent the easterly winds, and for that I am grateful to you. But now I need more. A ship. Now! How long do I have to wait? For Christ's sake, how much longer do you expect me to continue on this diet of stinking fish? Can't you see I am growing scales already? A ship—by the gods, send me a ship . . ."

Apr. 27   *97th day*
*Would you believe it: she has done it again! At dawn, as my
marvelous goddess blushingly disappeared behind the rising
sun, a ship spotted us; and today's date is 27—my lucky number and obviously her favorite also. The* Rhine Ore, *a German
freighter, after seeing my smoke flare, came straight at us: so
straight that, as I saw the ponderous bows looming high
above us—she was on ballast—I realized that her helmsman
had miscalculated, and we were about to be rammed. What
a way to end!*

10

To be rammed in broad daylight by a vessel that not only had seen us but was coming to our aid would have been the final irony. Yet there she was: her rusty, immense bows inexorably plowing a furrow of doom toward *Britannia*, helplessly lying broadside to her, less than half a cable away—fifty yards—twenty . . .

. . . *I rowed like mad and by a miracle managed to bring* Britannia *about as the bows passed a bare five yards from us, then kept trying to steer away while the* Rhine Ore *sped by—not fast, but enough to make me wish I had never seen her. She sucked us in until I could not use the starboard oar without hitting her side. Hoping the props would miss us, I pulled in the oar, cursing savagely at the stupidity of gods and men alike. As luck would have it, the swirl of the props pushed us away and we were O.K.—but, man, that was close!*

The Rhine Ore *finally stopped half a mile upwind and up-current from us. After I had spent half an hour trying to get somewhere near them, they finally realized what was going on and, gently backing their engines, drew nearer and passed me a rope. After that, it was sheer bliss. Everybody was most kind. I had a breakfast of four eggs and bacon and two cold beers, and they also gave me everything I needed except a couple of minor items that I forgot to ask for. Food and water for two weeks, as I did not wish to load* Britannia *again. By supplementing it with fish I can make it last for a month, and after that I will see. The captain promised to send some letters I had written, and also some film rolls for ITN. Also gave position as 21°41′ North, 45°15′ West. Now we are all set again. Thank you, Venus; with protection like yours I'll go through hell and come out unscathed.*
Rowed eleven hours.

Leaving the *Rhine Ore* and watching her disappear over the horizon had been in no way as painful as, say, leaving the *Skauborg*. Meeting her and exchanging a few words with other human beings had been pleasant, but somehow I regarded them as intruders upon the privacy of my little world. Going on board, shaking hands, sitting at a table to eat—the whole episode struck me as odd and unreal. It was as if I had stepped onto a different planet altogether. I very much needed the goods they could provide me with; but once these had been supplied I craved for the solitude that had been my own for so long, and I watched them go without sorrow. Loneliness was no longer a specter to be feared, but more a cherished companion without whom I was at a loss.

Apr. 28   *98th day*
Winds from the east, Force 3–4.
A little whale paid us a visit today. By "little" I mean slightly bigger than Britannia. *She kept swimming underneath us a bare two fathoms deep, and several times I went down and*

*touched her without in the least disturbing her lumbering
pace. Surrounded by the boys, she was quite a sight, and
again I regretted not having a camera suitable for underwater filming. She left after six or seven hours. The only
whale I had met so far.*

I had the first inkling of unusual company when, tossing a
cigarette end overboard, I absentmindedly followed its drift.
Suddenly a big, fast-moving shadow appeared underneath it,
so enormous that my first, instinctive reaction was to look up
at the sky to see if a passing cloud had obscured the sun. Just
then the whale surfaced to breathe, and I dived into the rathole for the camera. Unfortunately, although she stayed with
us for the rest of the day, she never again came up to breathe
at less than a cable away. Aside from that, she kept making
passes at *Britannia* from underneath, uttering funny, cooing
noises all the time, till I could have sworn she had fallen in
love with my *Britt*: a rather unnerving thought, and suddenly I wished I knew more about whales' courting habits.

As the hours passed without our whale's showing any sign
of leaving, I got more and more curious about her and, the
better to look, began to dive toward her as she swam under
Britannia's keel. At first I stopped a few feet short of the massive back, but eventually, seeing that she did not seem in the
least perturbed by my presence, I dared to give her a few
gentle taps. Still no response—whereupon my recklessness
turned insolent and, getting hold of the dorsal fin, I hitched a
short ride. Only once, though. She was not in the least put
out, don't think she even noticed—but all at once I was
frightened by my rashness, and I hurriedly returned to *Britannia*'s relative safety. After that, for no accountable reason,
I began to feel increasingly apprehensive at the whale's presence, earnestly wishing she would stop fooling around and
get on her way. At last she did, sometime during the night.
She was a very nice whale, really, and I do hope she finds
herself an equally likable, if more suitable, mate.

Apr. 29   *99th day*
Winds from the east, Force 3–4.
A hundred days today. How do I feel about it? I must say,
absolutely unexcited. The prospect of two more months, at
the very least, of the same is enough to dampen any sense of
achievement I might otherwise have felt. I am in excellent
physical shape, Britannia is a magnificent boat and, so far,
every bit of equipment has worked perfectly; but then the
sheer boredom of rowing twelve hours or so every day is beginning to get me down. I feel more like an animal than a
human being. A real galley slave. To enjoy life I need action
and excitement, and this rowing the Atlantic no longer pro-
vides it. The newness has gone from it, and every day is so
much like the others that it's almost nauseating. I have got
to think of something to liven this up, but what? Catching
sharks with a loop is no longer thrilling, and the same ap-
plies to everything else. What the hell can I do—apart from
rowing?*
Rowed twelve hours.

True, I was fully occupied, but always with the same
things. What I wanted was something different, a distraction, an accident—anything that would break the brutalizing
pattern of my days and nights. If I had become nervous
about the whale and wished her to leave, my joy at her appearance had turned sour only when she had overstayed her
welcome—a natural reaction considering her size and persistent attentions. An affectionate caress with her mighty tail
could have turned *Britannia* into smithereens, and I had no
means of defending her. The rotten truth was that I was beginning to feel thoroughly fed up with everything, myself included, and that was a dangerous state of mind.

The one bright spot of my day had been a bottle of wine, a
present my mother had brought to me in Las Palmas from my
Argentinian friends. The label was completely covered with

* An error I incurred by writing the Log past 2400 GMT.

the signatures of well-wishers, and I wallowed in pleasant nostalgia whilst deciphering them all. My mother had told me it was their wish that I toast their health on my one-hundredth day at sea—a pledge that I honored with great enjoyment. Thank you, my friends; it was damned good wine!

Apr. 30   *100th day*
Position 22°15′ North, 46°51′ West.
Today I have succeeded in rejoining the course I intended to follow when leaving Las Palmas. Three full months to the day since the winds sidetracked me from it. Naturally, I have no hope of following it as I would if I had a powerboat under my feet—but perhaps, barring a very bad spell of unfavorable winds, I shall be able to keep reasonably near to it. From now on I shall try to steer Britannia on a due-westerly course until we reach the island of Mayaguana and go through the Caicos Passage, then south a bit before starting the last leg to Florida, on a northwesterly course. I would like to approach Florida from the south because, according to the charts, there is a terrific current through the Florida Strait where the Gulf Stream flows at anything from thirty-three to sixty-eight miles per day. Obviously I must try and cut through it diagonally. These are my intentions at the moment; what will come out of them will be seen.
Rowed eleven hours.

May 1   *101st day*
Winds from the east, Force 4.
May already! Only two months to go—I hope. Today being the day of the workers, I suddenly, and for the first time in my life, felt in sympathy and decided to celebrate with them. Accordingly, I rowed only eight hours—some celebration! Apart from that, nothing happened. I spent my extra free hours sleeping.

May 2   *102nd day*
Winds from the east, Force 3–4.
I should feel somewhat refreshed today, but in fact I feel worse. Has it ever occurred to anyone what it is like to row twelve hours every day, and do everything else besides? I hardly feel as a person anymore. A galley slave, a beast of labor, a rowing machine—anything but a human being. If I go on, I might even lose sight of the whole reason for it all. My brain is so dulled by now by such tremendous physical exertion that my state of mind defies description; one just has to go through it to realize what it is like. Maybe one day, looking back on it, I may be able to depict the whole with clarity, but just now it is far beyond my capabilities. I still look the standard picture of health and fitness, but the vitality, the bouncing energy that has brought me so far, is seeping out of me. Already, and there is so much to go still!
Rowed twelve hours.

Restless, bounding from melodramatic bursts of heroic determination to fits of desperate, self-pitying misery, I had never been in such low morale. There was nothing wrong with the weather or the boat—in fact, nothing wrong at all, as for quite a while now things could hardly have gone better.

I was tired, tired, tired. If I went on it was only because there was nothing else to do, nowhere else to go. I had reached the most dangerous, crucial stage when, at the very limit of my endurance, something was bound to break. If it did so, at this point, I knew, or rather sensed, that the whole structure would collapse. On the other hand, if I managed to hold on till the crisis passed, I would emerge not only stronger, but almost indestructible. True or not, I simply had to believe that. Only a supreme confidence could pull me, so utterly alone, through my seemingly desperate quest.

May 3   *103rd day*
Winds from the east, Force 3.
*Beautiful easterly winds. Had them for so long now I have
forgotten what it is like to row against a contrary wind. I
suppose that makes me very lucky indeed. Venus, my lovely
goddess, where would I be without you? Because no man,
absolutely no one, could row single-handed across this part
of the Atlantic without drifting south unless he has the easterly winds I have had, and (let us not be overmodest about
it) rows as I have rowed and still am rowing. Still, no amount
of rowing would have allowed me to reach this longitude,
48° West, at this latitude, 22° North, without the easterlies.
May they blow forever! I need them now more than ever; I
am not so strong anymore. Oh, Florida, where are you?*
Rowed twelve hours.

May 4   *104th day*
*I shouldn't have mentioned the wind at all yesterday. Some-
how I get the feeling that every time I do, something happens. Is Venus playing with me? Today I have southerly
winds, Force 4. What will happen now is hard to say yet. I
guess I can stop worrying about losing latitude for the time
being, but I surely don't want to get too far north. Southeasterly now would have been ideal. What's more, according
to the Pilot Chart, that's the way it should blow, if at all.
Maybe I've had it too good for too long. Shouldn't complain
really, not yet.*
Rowed twelve hours.

May 5   *105th day*
Winds still from the south, Force 4.
*And I saw two UFOs shortly after sunset. Since I don't really
believe or disbelieve in such things, I will report without
comment. They appeared at 2330 GMT, my position being
approximately 22°40′ North, 49°19′ West, as two very bright
stars, about twice as bright as Venus, bearing 080 true. I was*

rowing at the time and almost directly facing them. The UFOs remained stationary, or very nearly so, for about five minutes at an altitude of approximately 20 degrees, fairly close together. The only bright star above them was Arcturus. They could not possibly have been stars, but I may as well mention it. They moved later toward the west, gaining altitude until they got about 15 degrees below and to the west of Jupiter, outshining it to the extent of making Jupiter look like a star of Magnitude plus-8 by comparison. At that moment a low rain cloud passed, obscuring every star, including Jupiter, that was in its way—except the UFOs.

For a while they moved erratically and then went east again, then lost altitude until they were touching the horizon almost. One of them shot upward then, climbing very fast toward Ursa Major, passed between Alioth and Dubhe (I mention all the stars by name because I don't want anybody to think that I confused UFOs with stars), swerved slightly toward Phecda and suddenly disappeared. When I looked down, searching for the other, it was also gone.

The whole show lasted about twenty minutes, more or less. They were not man-made satellites. I see satellites almost every night, and apart from the fact that none of them is by far so bright, satellites always follow a more or less straight course at the same speed.

Rowed eleven hours.

I know that most people will say, "Poor chap, the way he was feeling at the time, there is no doubt that he suffered a hallucination"—which, of course, I did not. Throughout the journey, whatever else I may have suffered, I never had hallucinations—except once perhaps, when I was very sick, but then I am not sure that that could be called a hallucination, as I recognized it as such. So, aside from what is reported in the Log, what else did, or do I imagine did, happen?

A very light breeze ruffled the sea. A few dark, rainy clouds scattered the sky. Since it was bright, still low and almost due east of me, I had chosen Arcturus to steer by, as this was easier and less tiring than keeping an eye on the compass all the time. After months of rowing at night, every night, the position of the stars was as familiar to me as the back of my hand. Thus, when the UFOs suddenly appeared, they immediately had my attention. Not only were they extraordinarily bright, but they were also blue and, to all appearances, they did not move. Amazing! Bewildered, I checked the time—2330 GMT—and bearing—080 true; then stopped rowing and watched them, wondering.

After a while they climbed toward Jupiter, at the time nearly overhead, and hovered there. How far? I could not say, except that it was at this moment that the rainy cloud passed without concealing them. They were, by then, as bright as street lamps, about five hundred yards apart. I lit a cigarette and watched them, mesmerized as the light grew brighter and brighter, almost to the point of hurting my eyes; yet their size did not vary—and incredible as it may sound, in spite of their increased brilliance, there was no reflection of light.

Something happened then about which I do not consciously remember anything other than a feeling that my body was floating in a void, or rather that I no longer had a body, as my whole being seemed to be struggling against a terrific, mental, esoteric force that was willing me to give myself to it, to say yes, to go away, to abandon myself. . . . It was so vivid, and yet so vague, vague. All I remember is the struggle, the resistance, and my saying "No, no. No." And then, at the last possible moment, when I was about to give in, I snapped out of it. The cigarette had burned, its entire ash completely unmoved, till it reached my fingers, and the burn had brought me back to my senses. I found myself absolutely bathed in sweat, and by the look and feel of them, my fingers must have been burning for quite a while before I had noticed. After that the UFOs went east again, and what happened then is in the Log.

Another tall story, by another one of those lone sailors?
Maybe. Think what you wish. Personally, I will take the easy
way out and say that I still don't believe or disbelieve in such
things. Or do I?

11

May 6   *106th day*
Winds from the south, Force 4.
*As I feared, I have been driven north—my position at sunset
being 22°54′ North, 49°42′ West. This would have made me
jump for joy a fortnight ago; now it's not so funny. I'm only
about a hundred and fifty miles from the northern limits of
the trades belt, and I sure have no wish to go through a new
edition of my first month at sea. Quite aside from the fact
that now I doubt very much that I have the strength left to
fight as I did then. Now when I hit the bunk, or what passes
for it in Britannia, I am as near dead as anyone can be without actually being a corpse. If the wind blows against me I
will have to go with it, wherever it takes me. I have no
choice.*
Rowed eleven hours.

May 7 107th day

It happened. Today I had westerly winds—only 2–3, but westerlies all the same. Squally and generally unsettled weather with a glassy color, rather calm. I don't have a barometer, but it has all the looks of a storm in the offing. It is terribly hot in spite of there being no sun, and the atmosphere is generally humid and extremely oppressive. Not at all as it is usually at sea, but more like the jungle. Che sarà sarà. Can't sleep because of the heat, and as I write this it is 0100 zone time. A ship is passing, all lights ablaze and so near I could almost touch it. Makes me feel full of nostalgia, and the temptation to light a flare and to hell with everything is very strong. Instead I switched off my torch, lest they see it, and watched it disappear. I shall soon be in the shipping lane that goes to South America, east coast, if I'm not in it already. Maybe I will stop a ship then and ask them for some goodies and cigarettes.
Rowed eleven hours.

May 8–15 108th–115th days

Afraid I have not been very good at keeping the diary up to date this last week. I usually write at night, just before going to sleep, 2400 hours zone time. But the night of the eighth I felt very sick. Of all things, I had a head cold complicated by diarrhea and general nausea. My temperature went up to 39° Centigrade* at one stage, and for two days I felt fit to die. Apart from that, my rash came back, and a big boil came out right where it rubbed the most. It is always the same with boils. If one wants to look one's best for a particularly interesting new date, ten to one a boil is likely to come out in the middle of one's nose. Rowing the Atlantic, where one couldn't care less what one looks like, it had to come out on the arse. I felt like giving up rowing altogether for a day or two; but in the battle of the spirit against

* 102.2° Fahrenheit.

the flesh, the spirit won once more, and I managed to put in eight hours a day until I felt better. That was the eleventh, when I resumed my schedule of twelve hours.

This is now the last stage, the hardest of all, with a hell of a lot more to go, and I feel that relaxing my self-imposed discipline would be disastrous if I want to reach Florida—and this I must. The West Indies are now within easy reach, relatively speaking, but all it will mean to me, once I pass 60° West Longitude, is that I will have successfully crossed the Atlantic. My real battle against the sea is still to be fought and won. It is a race now against the hurricane season. If a hurricane hits me, I have had it; in fact, the way I feel, I think I would go down in a gale, never mind a hurricane. After the seventh, by the way, when I thought one was coming, nothing happened, except a change of the wind, which went all around the card for twenty-four hours, then settled once more on the east. Today I am becalmed, and as it is too hot to row, I have stopped two hours earlier than usual, 1000 zone time. After finishing this I will try and sleep, as I will have to catch up with my rowing tonight.

Beautiful night for lovemaking, not rowing! However, rowed eleven hours.

May 16   *116th day*

Rowing. To row. I row. She rows. They row. No! Nobody but me rows. It means to make a boat move through the water by means of oars and oneself. One day, after I die and go to hell, I know what will happen: Satan will condemn me to row. I'm fed up, fed up—up to the balls with rowing. Ten hours today.

May 17   *117th day*

Running out of tobacco. Five, maybe six pipes is all. Bloody life!

Rowed eleven hours.

May 18   *118th day*
Wind coming strong from the east. Rain. Nothing happens—
nothing but me rowing. Twelve hours.

May 19   *119th day*
Bad weather, latterly from the east. Overcast, squalls, winds
5–6. Life very uncomfortable, but should be making very
good time. Britannia flies with the waves at what must be at
least four knots. Am rowing only ten hours today.

May 20   *120th day*
Still bad. Same as yesterday. Tomorrow is my birthday, and
I hope it will improve a little. Four months today, and such
a long way to go still.
Rowed ten hours.

May 21   *121st day*
My birthday, and one of the worst days at sea. I ran out of
tobacco; had a bit for half a pipe only, which I had kept to
celebrate—and it got wet. A tin of raspberries I had also
kept for today gassed and I had to throw it away. And just
as I was about to have a sip of brandy to celebrate my birth-
day, an enormous wave, about fifteen feet high, hit Britannia
squarely broadside and washed me overboard. Lost the
bottle and hurt my leg and foot very badly. Had my last
meal from the Rhine Ore stores—from tomorrow it will be
fish and rice again till the next ship. Apart from that, a very
happy birthday!
Rowed eight hours.

Thirty-two years that felt like a hundred. Of all the things
that happened I did not know which hurt most—the indignity of being washed overboard, mangling my leg, losing the
brandy or getting the last scraps of tobacco wet.

Britannia was drifting, unhappily riding the slopes of ten-foot waves. Battered and ravaged by the sea, her gay, bright orange color scraped and bleached into a dirty, nondescript yellow, she looked positively sick. Poor thing, she had come a long way—learning a few lessons, as well as teaching me some. Veteran of a thousand tumbles, as proved by her many scars, she had finally accepted that the sea, not I, was her enemy. We were both tired, sick, scarred—and proud of it: of what we had done together, of what we could still do. In the last few days, swirling in an angry mass of gray water, we had become so used to the dangers and discomforts that we no longer paid attention to the resentful snarls and hisses of breaking waves. Would this one go under, or would it swamp us? Who cared!

It was in this don't-give-a-damn mood that I was standing on deck, the uncorked bottle of brandy in my hands, musing on an appropriate toast to fit the occasion, when I suddenly saw the wave coming. It was so enormous that for a moment, I refused to trust my eyes. Unbelieving, I gaped at it, watched it come, swell, rise high above us, where it stood, seemingly poised for a second or two, as the ponderous crest reared on itself, flexing, arching . . .

Snapping out of my incredulous immobility, I jumped headlong, in a desperate, last-minute dive, for refuge in my rathole. Too late! Plunging with a hard, devastating blow on *Britannia*'s unprotected deck, what must have been tons of churning, foamy water crushed me against it, tossing me around like a bit of flotsam—and all I could think of was not losing the brandy.

Next thing I knew, I was in the water—spitting, spluttering, sore from head to foot, clutching the brandy bottle as if for dear life, with my thumb pressed hard against the uncorked neck to keep the sea from mixing with its precious contents. Fortunately, I had been washed overboard on the lee side, and carried by the waves, *Britannia* soon came to my rescue, allowing me to grab the gunwale and haul myself back on board.

A quick inspection showed that nothing was missing—
everything having been firmly lashed down, as is usual in bad
weather. All was as it should be, and I could easily have dismissed the whole incident, except for two things: In spite of
my efforts, saltwater had found its way inside the brandy
bottle, and the resulting cocktail was positively undrinkable.
Also, my leg had been hurt, rather badly. I was lucky in a
way, as no bones had been broken—but as birthday presents
go, this was a kind I could well have done without. Oh hell!
Somehow I had to find a way to celebrate. Sleep seemed to
be the only solution. But how can one sleep if, every five
minutes or so, the bunk becomes a bathtub and one starts
floating away from it?

May 22   *122nd day*
Winds from the east, 5, 6, gusting to 7. Rains and seas very
rough. Have not been able to spearfish and ate a bit of rice
only; very hungry. My leg is all blue and hurts terribly. The
sole of my right foot, where I hit it against the edge of the
sliding seat, is a mess. A chunk of flesh the size of a very
large bean has burst out and looks like a sausage when the
skin is split and the meat comes out. Wonder what is going
to happen to it? Never had a wound like this before. Will it
rot, dry up or be reabsorbed? Wounds don't heal well at
sea, and I can hardly keep my foot dry. If it starts to rot, I
will have to cut it away, I guess. Once in South America I
was hunting alone and had to dig out a poisonous thorn from
my thigh. It was about an inch deep, and I had to bite on
a piece of wood to prevent myself from screaming while I
dug. By the time I had finished I was about to pass out, the
pain had been so ferocious. So I know that if it comes to cut-
ting it I'll have the kind of guts it takes to do the job, but I
certainly don't relish the idea. Tried to row, but it proved
impossible; my leg just won't take the strain. Forced to drift.
Luckily, the wind is easterly.

I was having a bad time. Not only did sea and sky seem to have joined forces to make life impossible—it rained all the time now, practically nonstop—but even my faithful dolphins became uncooperative. Not that they had deserted us, but for some unfathomable reason, they refused to come within shooting distance of the spear gun. Jerrycan was the only one who kept coming—peering at me, probably wondering why I had stopped feeding him. I told him that if his brothers didn't start cooperating soon, the time would come when *he* would feed *me*. A fistful of rice was all I had left, and by staying around so much, Jerrycan was stretching our friendship to a dangerous degree. Without tobacco, cold, wet, my leg screaming with pain every time I banged it against something, needlessly putting up with hunger as well was a bit much.

May 23   *123rd day*
Winds from the east, Force 5–6.
Leg a bit better today—still blue, but swelling gone. My wound looks all right, but flesh still hanging out; I just can't walk and must crawl around.
Rowed six hours. Absolute hell.
Again no fish today; very hungry. Come on Venus—give me a hand.

Jerry was not around. Driven by despair at his stupidity, I had clubbed him with an oar, and he was gone. Would I ever see him again?

May 24   *124th day*
Got a dolphin at last. My leg is better, but the foot still hurts badly. It throbs away and feels very hot to the touch. I can, however, row by putting all the pressure on the left one— uncomfortable, but it can do. Wonder where I am? Been overcast since the fifteenth, and I have had no chance of taking a sight. Still raining continuously, and the sea gray and

menacing. Everything damp or outright soaked. Life most miserable. However, my morale is now much higher than a week or so ago. Nothing like troubles and difficulties to bring out the fighting spirit in me. Must have a masochistic streak somewhere. All the same, the sea has apparently decided to give me a battle, and by the gods, this is what I'm out here for.

May 25   *125th day*
Everything is a bit better today, my foot included. I am still half crippled—but never mind, it will pass. Got a couple of stars through the clouds, and my position is 22°55′ North, 60°50′ West: extraordinarily good average, in spite of my poor rowing. The wind really made us go. And having passed Longitude 60, I consider myself as having crossed the Atlantic. So far, so good. Beware now, Florida, here I come!

Incredibly, in the last ten days my average had been a fantastic forty miles per day. My best time so far—and because of my injured leg, rowing had had very little to do with it. True, out of a possible two hundred and forty hours, I had manned the oars for ninety-two, but my rowing had been rather sloppy, and I had devoted my efforts more to steering than to anything else. The fact that I was never again able to repeat this performance shows what a great help a strong wind can be—provided, of course, it comes from the right quarter. Unfortunately, the misery that such weather brought was far too great, and the eight or ten extra miles per day were not really worth such a price. All the same, we were getting on, and that was what mattered most. The West Indies were now only a few hundred miles to the south of us. Had I so wished, I could have been stepping ashore by now. Antigua, Martinique, Barbados, it would not have mattered. Who could have accused me of not having crossed the Atlantic? Instead, after one hundred and twenty-five days at sea, because of a whim I still had twelve hundred miles to go!

How many more days? Would I ever see land, any land, again? And if I did, and it was not Florida, would I have the fortitude, the determination, the madness to go on? That would be the final test. If I could resist the temptation to end my journey then and there, then surely, even if I never did reach Florida and the sea finally managed to destroy me, would I not, nevertheless, have won?

May 26   *126th day*
Rain again. It never used to rain before; now it is one squall after another. Used to enjoy it at the beginning, when I had marvelously refreshing showers getting rid of months of accumlated salt, but now it is a bit too much. The wind has changed; from the south now, but very light: Force 2–3. Still, it will make us drift to the north—I hope not too much. Rowed ten hours.

May 27   *127th day*
My lucky date, only this time it failed me in a most miserable way. The wind today is from the southwest—barring a westerly, the very worst wind for us—Force 3, 4, 2, and rain, rain day and night. Made very little progress. I feel tired and hungry. I hate fish so much by now, I don't think I will ever eat it again for the rest of my life—once I get out of this, that is.
Rowed ten hours.

Fish! What a stinking word that is! Lifesaving, since I have nothing else. I eat a hell of a lot of it—have to if I want to keep my energy: five, maybe six pounds a day. Boiled, raw, dried, it doesn't matter how I try to prepare it; the result is always the same: nauseating. I eat as much as I can, actually forcing myself to swallow more than my stomach can reasonably hold, yet I am always hungry. I have known real hunger before, but never in such a peculiar way. Because if one fills one's belly to the point of bursting, one should not feel hungry all the time, as I do. Apparently there are simply not enough calories in six pounds of fish to replace what I burn. But if I try to eat any more, and I have, I only succeed in vomiting, feeling sick and hungrier than before. It is getting so bad I find myself wishing I had some of Archie's stuff left. A turtle would make my day, but there aren't any to be seen. Maybe tomorrow.

May 28   *128th day*
Southwesterly winds still, Force 3–4.
Very bad. I can see it all happen again, as in the first days after I left the Canaries. The sea—I've decided she's a frigging female—has it against me in the most stupid way. Time by now she realized that she hasn't got a hope in hell of tiring me out to the point of giving up. If it takes me a year, I'll get to Florida. The only way she can stop me is by sending me to the bottom in a hurricane. So let's have it—either send me one, or stop this nonsense and let me have some fair winds. God damn it! What's the use! Females! Bah!
Rowed ten hours.

Females! I have been asked many times what it was like to spend six months alone at sea without even the soft purrs of a doe-eyed little thing to keep my mind off rowing.

"Well," I say, "If you don't see, or hear, or smell them, then you don't miss them."

Rot! The honest truth be told, the way I felt most of the time, I could have ravaged all of King Solomon's harem twice over, and still gone back for more. When I think of all those magnificent, burning sunsets, those beautiful, warm, starry nights—ye gods, and all I had to rest my weary hands on was a bleeding pair of oars! Let me tell you, at those times, knowing that my beloved Venus waited for me, somewhere in the mysterious recesses of her cloudy alcove, was no consolation, none at all. But what's the use. Females—wow!

May 29   *129th day*
Southwesterlies still.
Tired out of this world. My foot is practically as good as new.
The little bit of flesh has now been reabsorbed by the sausage, and although I still cannot step on it, there are almost no signs left of the wound. Am very pleased with being such a healthy bastard. I have been able to sleep only very little and, as I said before, feel extremely tired. Have the idea that I have been making no progress at all—and I'm still hungry. What would I do to get a big juicy steak! Venus, my beloved, I need you again. Do something for me and stop this bloody sea from being such an idiot. And what about a ship, too?
Rowed eleven hours.

May 30   *130th day*
I couldn't believe my eyes, but there it was: a beautiful ship coming straight at me. Canadian Pacific Lines. Stopped for only half an hour. They were on charter and not very pleased about it. Got a few things from them—mainly water and perishable food, including so much cheese I really don't know what I'm going to do with it. All the same, it was marvelous, and after they left, I stuffed myself to the point of bursting. Now I'm feeling terribly sick, and also have fever.
Rowed six hours.

Captain Peter Roberts was far from pleased at the scraggly sight of *Britannia* bobbing up and down alongside his huge ship, and made very few bones about it. Since I had not been invited to climb aboard, I had sent up, at the end of a heaving line, my "shopping list," as he called it later. Propped against the railings, his face creased in a deep frown of concentration, he was trying to decipher the hastily scribbled note. A particular item caught his attention.

"Shampoo?" he screamed. "What in the name of God do you want shampoo for?"

"Why, Captain, to wash my hair, of course. What do you think?" I yelled back.

He shook his head and told his chief steward to get everything I was asking for: "On the double, do you hear? On the double!" Then he leaned back toward me. "Do you know, young fellow, that this ship is on charter and that every hour I lose will cost my company a thousand dollars? Who's going to pay for it? Hey?"

"I didn't hear that, Captain. Would you mind repeating, please?"

"You are crazy!"

"Aye, aye, Captain. How about some water? I need some water too. Think you could let me have some?"

"Water? To drink? Or to wash your hair with?"

"To drink, please."

"Anything else?"

"Well, yes. As a matter of fact, I could use some pipe tobacco and a carton of cigarettes—preferably tipped ones."

I thought he would blow a fuse, but he disappeared from sight before I could tell him the particular brand I had in mind.

Eventually, they left in such a hurry that I was nearly caught in the propellers' wash; but—and I must say this for Captain Roberts—he blew the horn three times in salute, and that is something one does not forget, ever.*

I had asked mainly for canned food, but found myself with a supply of perishable stuff—cheese, butter, eggs and bread —for which I had such a terrible craving that I ate and ate and ate. I should have known better, but couldn't resist the temptation. It did not kill me, but only just.

* I met Captain Roberts again in London. We later became friends, and with his charming wife, Jeannie, he gave me the pleasure and honor of being present at the launching of *Britannia II*, the boat in which, by the time this book sees the light, I hope to be rowing the Pacific, from San Francisco to Australia.

May 31 and June 1   *131st and 132nd days*

Been very ill, with high temperature, and feeling weak as a baby. Have not rowed at all and, at one time yesterday, nearly went off my head. In fact, I did. As I was vomiting over the side, a shark came by and started swimming around Britannia in lazy circles. A tiger shark, looking very mean, and as I stared at it, an overpowering hate slowly began to boil up inside me and suddenly, screaming like a madman, I pulled out my knife and dived at it. Luckily, the shark did not seem interested and slowly swam away, with me in hot pursuit. I don't know for how long this went on, but finally the shark sounded and disappeared—and as I came to my senses and looked around, for a while I could not see Britannia. Finally, I was on top of a swell and saw her about five hundred yards from me, drifting away. It was my great fortune that at the time there was barely a whisper of wind; otherwise I would never have been able to catch up with her. Venus really must have been looking after me.

When I made it back and climbed over the side, little lights seemed to twinkle all around me. I was still swimming and there was fog and I could not see anything and Britannia was drifting away and then the white belly of the shark appeared and stood between me and Britannia and I plunged and slashed at it, cursing and yelling as I felt the blade go through, tearing, ripping, again and again. Then I regained my senses and saw I had been slashing at the white canvas of my rain catcher, and I just stared at it—then crawled into my rathole and lay down pounding the deck with my fists, until finally I cried myself to sleep. I can't remember ever before in my life breaking down like that, and I hope it does not happen again. It is most unpleasant.

Today I still feel bad, but not quite so much as yesterday. There is no wind whatsoever; the sea is like a mirror, and it is very hot.

Did not row at all.

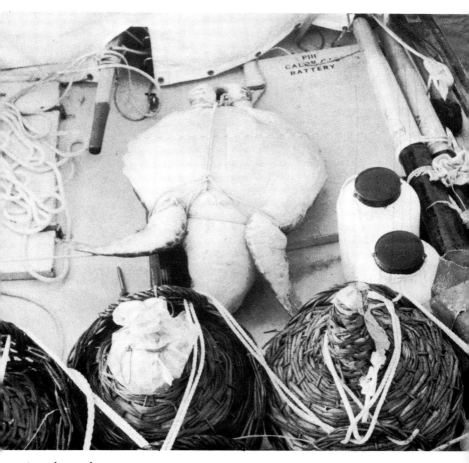

A turtle caught at sea.

A plane carrying newsmen lands near *Britannia,* Great Bahama Bank.

To gorge myself with rich food had been a terribly serious mistake—all the more so since I knew damn well at the time I shouldn't do it. It was easy to find excuses, to tell myself that I would have had to be more than human not to yield to the temptation. A few days and most of my treasure would have spoiled. Yet the fact remained that I had willfully broken a cardinal rule of survival by, in my case, an unpardonable lack of willpower.

Now, feeling so frail I could barely stand, my stomach quivering in relentless spasms of pain, I feelingly cursed myself for the dolt I was—while *Britannia* quietly drifted along. And I cursed, too, because the sea was so calm, so frighteningly, unnaturally calm, that I felt, perhaps as never before, the awesome immensity of my solitude.

June 2   *133rd day*
Finally got through to London after trying for nearly a fortnight. This made me quite happy. Still feel shaky, and the rowing made me dizzy, but half an hour at a time, I managed to row five hours. Slight breeze from the east.

June 3   *134th day*
Wind from the east, 2–3.
Feeling better; rowed six hours.

June 4   *135th day*
Today the dolphins had a tragic encounter. We met a school of about fifty porpoises, the first I've seen since starting. They bore down on Britannia with high, squeaking noises and attacked my boys without a moment's hesitation. It was a terrible slaughter. I'm sure that most of the bigger dolphins could have escaped, but they seemed to consider Britannia as home, therefore a secure place. They all grouped around and under her, and the porpoises had a field day. When I

*dived to look at the battle from below there were only ten
left out of at least a hundred. They were in a row, flat against
Britannia's bottom, and didn't dare to move as the porpoises
circled around; and every now and then one charged the
closely packed bunch, grabbing one and scattering the rest,
although barely so, as they immediately regrouped in their
position under Britannia. Eventually only three were left,
and the porpoises stopped paying attention to them, turning their curiosity toward me. They circled me, squeaking
and nudging one another, until, after five minutes, they
swam away and soon disappeared. It was most interesting.
Of the three surviving dolphins one looked a bit, mangled,
and I speared him for dinner tomorrow. All in all, a very bad
day for them.*
Rowed five hours.

It was hard to believe that Jerrycan and my boys were no
more. They had kept us company for so long that I could
hardly believe I would never see them again. Others would
come, presumably, but my boys had had a personality all of
their own, and it would never be the same without Jerrycan.
I wondered what had happened to him? Since the day I had
bashed him with the oar I had not seen him again. I would
never know, of course, but it was nice to think that today he
had not been among the others. As a curious aftermath, I
noticed that no shark whatever appeared in the vicinity.
Considering the amount of blood and scattered flesh left by
the carnage, one would have thought the sea would be alive
with them, but none came.

June 5   *136th day*
*I am eating as much as I can and recovering energy fast. I
feel now almost O.K. Still worrying a little, though, because
I still need rest.*
Rowed only five hours today.

June 6   *137th day*
Have been sighted by another ship today, the Bay Ross, *a
Norwegian. Went on board and got some canned goods. The
captain was most kind, and now I am all right with food and
tobacco. Unfortunately, my hammerhead trophy bumped
against the ladder of the* Bay Ross *and sank to the bottom.
After all the time I had spent working on it, I was really
sorry to lose it.*
*My position is only 63°30′ West. A very poor average since
I was ill, but now I feel well again and hope to improve. For
one thing, I have rowed eight hours today and tomorrow
hope to row more.*

On May 25 my position had been 60°50′ West. In the
twelve days since then I had managed to cover only about
one hundred and forty-five miles. Such an incredibly poor
average in generally rather good weather shows, perhaps
more than anything else, the difference between sailing and
rowing. The lone sailor who find himself unfit through sick-
ness or injury can always hope nonetheless to maintain a
steady rate of progress. A rower in the same condition may
consider himself extremely lucky if he doesn't lose ground.
The rower is the sails, the engine, the very life of his boat. If
he does not man the oars, he will drift aimlessly. Confronted
with the impossibility of rowing through simple lack of
strength, knowing how puny one's efforts are even at best,
can have a shattering impact on morale. It is very easy then
to understand why so many castaways lose all hope and
allow themselves to die, pervaded by a feeling of helplessness so intense it seems to merge with the ocean, whose vast-
ness then loses all boundaries, to become really and truly infinite. To overcome this feeling, to deny the existence of
infinity when one is not only surrounded by it but part of it
is, I think, one of the hardest tests man's spirit can encounter.
But then, I know of no greater satisfaction than that afforded
by such a triumph.

June 7   138th day
Rowed ten hours.

June 8   139th day
A stormy day, but the wind, Force 6–7, is from the east. This is good, but life again a misery. Will it ever end?

June 9   140th day
Heard on the radio that there was a tropical depression gathering strength in the Caribbean. Or, in plain language, that a hurricane was forming—but what the blighter didn't say is where, and what course it is supposed to follow. Have not been able to get any more information all day. I'll just have to hope for the best and, whatever its course, that I won't be in it.
Wind from the east, 4–5. Rain.
Rowed eleven hours.

June 10   141st day
Well, according to the news this morning, I am in the clear, as it hit Cuba and the south part of Florida, and I'm still far from there. It is a very cheerful thought that I shall soon be moving at my faster-than-light speed along the path followed by most hurricanes that form in the Caribbean, and that I shall be in it for many a day. Lucky I am, but how much can one ask? I'm going to be hit by one, I can feel it in my bones, and the only way to prevent it is to relinquish Florida for the Bahamas. Yet how can I do that after so much fighting and struggling? I'm not in the least suicide-minded, and the barest common sense suggests that I will be asking for it if I go on through the end of June and the first half of July. After all, I have crossed the Atlantic, haven't I? Why then be such a mule? The gods will surely be tempted if I go on and the sea is waiting to pounce. I will think about it and decide tomorrow.

Still raining. Wind from the east, Force 4–5.
Rowed twelve hours.

Many years ago, when I was working as first mate on the
Orion, a fishing ship in the Caribbean, we had been hit by a
hurricane—Anna, the first of the season. Actually, what hit
us was her fringe, the center passing some eighty-odd miles
to the north of us. All the same, the force of her blows was
such that the *Orion*, a converted German minesweeper, did
not stand a chance as she lay at anchor in the reef-protected
bay of one of the Serranilla cays.

It was at dawn, a dawn the like of which I had never seen
before, that Anna made her presence felt. The captain ordered everybody to abandon ship.

The air was hot, gray, oppressive. The cay, a barren patch
of sand, grass and rocks, half a mile long by three hundred
yards at its widest, maybe ten feet above sea level at its high-
est point, had almost disappeared under a carpet of seabirds.
Man-o'-wars, sea gulls, boobies and whatnot were all bun-
dled together in a nervous, whitish, feathery carpet. There
must have been thousands of them, and their frenzied ca-
cophony had to be heard to be believed. Mountainous clouds
hovered above, the blackness of the sky matching that of the
sea. Yet not a whisper of wind; not a ripple stirred the
waters. Then the first gusts of wind swept over us, accompa-
nied by a thundering rumble, as ominous as it was distant.
Within half an hour, pandemonium had broken loose.

Lashed by winds of up to ninety miles an hour, our little
cay became a swirling mass of sand, birds and water. Rain or
sea, it was impossible to say. Everything that had not been
solidly lashed or weighted down was swept away. We saved
ourselves by huddling, with a few hundred birds, in a little
gully behind an outcrop of rocks.

The *Orion* was wrecked in the first hour. She fought
bravely but, alone and helpless, what could she do? The little

lagoon became a boiling caldron, and the sea pounced on her from all sides, mercilessly battering her into submission, all the time pushing her with relentless determination toward the reef that protruded murderously at the far end of the cay. Like a wild thing suddenly come alive, she strained and tossed and reared against her chains, while the anchors dragged, stopped, then dragged again. For a moment, I thought she would make it when, in a last desperate effort, she managed to swerve toward the passage that would have taken her to a decent grave in the deep, open sea. It was not to be. In a paroxysm of fury, the sea exploded under her keel —lifting her almost clear out of the water, then letting her go, with a sickening thump, right on top of the reef. It was terrible to see one's ship die like that. Terrible, yet magnificent. How can destruction be so grandiose in its beauty as to be obscene—and remain beautiful?

Aye, I knew now what a hurricane was like and had no illusions as to what fate awaited *Britannia* should our paths cross again.

12

June 11   142nd day
Weather the same. Everything is just as wet, and I'm beginning to grow mushrooms: decidedly not the time to make up
my mind as to whether or not I should take a chance with a
hurricane. In any case, there is nothing I can do about it at
present, as I cannot follow any other course than the one I
am on—which should take me to the Turks Islands, and I
must be going really well.
With plenty of food, I now feel much stronger. I really eat
like a monster. In high, if damp, spirits.
Rowed twelve hours.

June 12   143rd day
Squall after squall is my lot. At home must be winter now,
and my mum is probably sitting in front of the fireplace

thinking about her crazy son. It is not a thing I yearn for very often, but today I really wish I were home, lying in front of that very fireplace—a glass of wine punch in my hand; a beautiful girl sprawled all over me, purring. Gee, how many times I have done so—and yet, at the end, I always got bored with it and wished I were where I am now, or in some similar situation. I must be indeed crazed. Guess that to really enjoy life I must have both. Now, when all this ends, I will again be able to enjoy the pleasures of life: the sophisticated as well as the very simple ones, like a shower or sleeping in a decent bed. They will have real meaning then. In fact, to be able to enjoy as a luxury the little things one has always taken for granted is perhaps the greatest pleasure of all. I shall get bored with it again, of course, but while it lasts it will be paradise. I would like to go hunting, too; I'm fed up with the sea. It's been a long time now, far too much of the same. Oh well, let's get on with it; then it will end.

Rowed twelve hours.

June 13   *144th day*
Thirteenth, and Friday to boot! Wonder what will happen today. Wind from the southeast, Force 4–5; overcast, no rain —about time.
Amazingly, nothing bad happened today. A school of porpoises paid us a visit, but stayed around only a few minutes. Winds are still coming strongly from the east-southeast. I am making excellent progress.
Rowed eleven hours.

June 14   *145th day*
Weather same. Wind from east, 4–5. Rain again. This is very uncomfortable, but for rowing very good. When it is not overcast, the heat is usually too great to allow me to row during the daytime. So all in all, I'm satisfied with the

*weather up to now, as long as the wind doesn't get stronger
—for that would be too much.*
Rowed eleven hours.

Up to date my fortune, as far as the equipment was concerned, had been incredible. True, I had always been extremely careful, taking great pains to see that everything
was, at all times, out of harm's way. Still, in an open boat the
size of *Britannia*, this was easier undertaken than done.
When the generator refused to start, my first reaction was
"This is it! It's been nice having you, but now I might as well
get rid of you." Without the generator I could not recharge
the batteries. No batteries, no radio, no more talks with London. The temptation to throw the lot overboard, further
lightening *Britannia* a hundred pounds, was almost overwhelming. Getting through to London every five days had
become a nightmare. Owing to a leak in its hydraulic system,
the aerial would simply not stay up any more than a few
minutes at a time. When it fell down I had to pump it up
again, at an average of once every three minutes. The mad
back-and-forth scramble every few minutes during the hour
it usually took before I could get through with London was
so frustrating that no amount of sweet talk from the other
side could alleviate it. Now I had a genuine reason for putting an end to it. One more call, with whatever juice was left
in the batteries, to report the situation, and away with everything! After all, everybody knew that as far as mechanics and
electricity were concerned, I was hopeless. If need be, most
of my friends would be more than happy to testify that I
don't know one end of a screwdriver from the other. I made
up my mind: the generator was going, and so was everything
else.

However, to assuage my conscience, I decided to make an
effort and, with the tools supplied by the manufacturer, took
the generator to pieces. Without the slightest idea of which
end to start from, I went about it by the straightforward,

uncomplicated system of loosening and pulling apart everything that could be loosened and pulled apart. The only
thing I didn't touch was the electrical side, or what I thought
had something to do with electricity. I had the darned thing
stripped in about an hour, which was not bad; then managed
to put everything back together—in four! I'd never thought I
could do it, and the fact that I was left with only a couple of
screws and nuts for which, much as I racked my brains, I
could not find a place left me with a tremendous feeling of
satisfaction. After that, to make sure that I was doing everything according to the book, I gave the damned thing a good
kick, then pulled the cord, and . . . as the motor fired into
life—first go, by the gods!—I nearly fell overboard with the
shock. From then on, I never had any more problems with
the generator. Let me add that the only reason I have mentioned this episode is that of all the unlikely things I have
done in my life, fixing the generator ranks amongst those of
which I feel proudest.

June 15   *146th day*
This morning I made a sort of little hook with a pin and
caught about a dozen tiny fish from a school that was swarm-
ing all around Britannia. *They are much tastier than big ones*
and, fried with onions (the onions are from the Bay Ross),
made a delicious breakfast. I seem to be always hungry.
Rowing must burn a lot of energy, but I am now eating very
well and don't think I am losing much weight. In fact, I am
again in excellent physical condition; I suppose that being
so near the end of my journey helps a lot. Still haven't made
up my mind about Florida, but a hundred to one I will go
on. We'll see.
Rowed ten hours.

Since the day of the dolphins' massacre by the porpoises,
Britannia had been left more or less alone. In fact, except for
a few prowling dolphins and sharks, no big fish seemed at-

tracted by her anymore. With plenty of food I did not particularly mind, but it was, nevertheless, rather sad. I missed
Jerrycan and the antics of the dorados more than I cared to
admit, and kept hoping for another school to join us. However, up to now, no such luck.

June 16   *147th day*
An American aircraft carrier stopped by this afternoon, the
Saratoga. *I was sleeping at the time. It was quite amazing
for me to scramble out of my rathole and see such a beautiful, gigantic fighting ship pass by. It was like a reminder of
the first big tanker I had met, the* Bulford. *They sent food
to me by helicopter. The funny thing about this is that they
lowered a lifeboat and came all the way down to me, as I
drifted downwind from the stopped vessel, and none of us,
neither the chap in charge of the lifeboat nor I, suggested
that I be towed back to the* Saratoga *and be given the food
there. Instead they sent a helicopter and dropped the food
a few feet from* Britannia. *Generous as usual, the Americans
really overdid it a bit. In fact, it was so heavy I could barely
pull it inside* Britannia *and later on had to throw some overboard. But it was a very nice thing for the captain to do—I
mean, to stop the* Saratoga *for me—and he also sent a personal gift: a carton of Raleigh cigarettes (I suppose he chose
Raleigh with a sense of humor) and a few other things and
goodies.*
*Well, Captain O'Neill, thank you very much. This is not only
from me but also from* Britannia, *because I'm sure she felt
very proud that such a big fighting ship should stop and
send a helicopter for little her. This was soon after noon.
Now the weather has changed: we are becalmed, and under
an incredibly moonless, starry sky.*
Rowed all night, about twelve hours, until dawn.

June 17   *148th day*
Becalmed. Not a whisper of wind, and infernally hot. Row-

*ing impossible. Shall have to wait till night. Need to sleep
anyway.*
*A most beautiful night. The sea is as calm as a lake. Rowing
is almost a pleasure. Almost—because I have been doing it
for too long now to enjoy it anymore. All the same, it's not
bad. However, I'm not likely to make much progress; I feel
lazy, and without a good wind aft my speed is reduced by
at least a knot. A night like this makes me feel at peace with
my mind—and I have decided that come what may, Florida's mine. I have no doubts about it now, and I'm beginning
to lose interest in this caper. In fact, I spend most of the
time, while rowing, thinking and planning my next one. By
the beginning of 1970—if all goes well—we shall see.*
Rowed ten hours.

In the absence of wind, the temperature during the day
would go up to and hover between 90° and 100° Fahrenheit.
Whenever this happened, life became an inferno. My rathole, the only place where I could hide from the sun, was a
veritable oven, and a few hours sleeping in it would sap my
energy almost as much as, if not more than, if I had been rowing. When I couldn't sleep, I lay in a state of torpidity, rivu-
lets of sweat forming all over my body, slowly and ticklishly
trickling down to form a sticky puddle underneath. When it
became unendurable I would go out for a swim, or simply
hang on to *Britannia*'s gunwale until a prowling shark forced
me to crawl back on board. The hours would drag forever as
I softly cursed the day I had ever thought of rowing across
the Atlantic.

Night at last. For a few hours the whisper of the sea
against *Britannia*'s hull as we doggedly plodded on, the rusty
squeaks of the sliding seat, the regular, rhythmic *plump-
thump* of the oars were a relief—a pleasure almost. Every
now and then the sudden splash of a big fish somewhere in
the distance would spark a living note in the otherwise ca-
daverous expanse of the sea.

"*Stars twinkle above . . .*" Had I imagined it, or had I heard a voice singing, far away? Painful illusions would stab at my solitude: someone was breathing hard at my back, almost touching me with barely suppressed gasps of burning passion, ready to change, as I knew too well, into sobs of anguish, or a derisive cackle, the moment I turned my head. The prelude of insanity? No: I had been at sea too long, that was all, and I was tired. Too God-damned tired.

As the hours dragged into the night, delusions, or illusions, would fade till mind and body became insensitive to everything other than a mantle of jaded, timeless weariness. The world became a lifeless, somber nothingness into which *Britannia* sluggishly plodded on and on and on, night after night, and what ever made me do it and kept me at the oars I shall never know.

June 18, 19 and 20   *149th, 150th and 151st days*
Left three days to pass without writing as there was absolutely nothing to write about and still the same. Calm, hot, boring. Have been able to get myself into an excellent position to cross the Caicos Passage, and this fills me with pleasure. I wanted to go through it as far back as the end of April, and succeeding in doing so is no mean feat. I am now choosing an almost exact position and then trying to get there. In this way the challenge is still there and I'm out to shame the sea as thoroughly as I can, by going exactly where I want to go.

I was not being facetious. To overcome the lassitude that was beginning to engulf me, I absolutely needed the tangible satisfaction of achieving a day-by-day goal. Florida was so far away still that unless I aimed my will at some more definite target, I was in danger of losing my grip on the sense of purpose that had allowed me to come so far. To have let three days go without writing the Log already showed a break in my discipline. That nothing had happened was irrelevant: what could happen, anyway? In my mind I had already crossed the Atlantic and that was that; but I had to reach Florida, didn't I? I could not give up, not now. But I wanted to. Oh, how I wanted to! Nothing but sea and sky for five months! Would it ever end?

June 21 and 22   *152nd and 153rd days*
Thought I was going through the Caicos Passage fine, but on fixing my position today, I find I have been pushed too far north by the southeast winds. Now it's too hot to row and I will have to wait till night. Not unduly perturbed, because it was partially my fault for being shoddy on my rowing— not making enough allowance to offset the wind while shaping my course. In any case, I'm still in a very good position for crossing, just southeast of Mayaguanas Island—more east than south, really.
I am now rowing exclusively at night and, for a couple of hours, just after and before dawn and sunset. At 0900 zone time it's already so hot that rowing becomes impossible, so I sleep—or try to sleep—during the day and row at night— which is terribly tedious, and I have to watch myself all the time or I suddenly find myself rowing thirty or forty degrees off course.

June 23   *154th day*
Wind from the northeast, Force 3. Excellent! Overcast and stormy during the night, with the wind gusting up to Force 5. Heaps of rain.

June 24   *155th day*
Going on fine. Losing latitude I think, but cannot check because of overcast. Rowing day and night; very tired. Rains continually, off and on.

The weather change was a gift from the gods when I needed it most. The drop in temperature and plentiful rain sparked new life in me. The rain was most welcome since I had been drinking three to four gallons of water every day during the previous week and, as I had not bothered to distill any during that time, my supplies were running short. Now I concentrated all my energies into navigating through the Caicos Passage.

The Caicos is about twenty miles wide, and it was my intention to go through it without sighting land—not trusting myself at this stage as to what my reactions might be if I physically saw land. It was bad enough to know it was but a few miles either side of my course. The temptation to row ashore might have proved too great, and I dedicated all my energies to rowing and navigation.

Since my last fix, two days before, I had had to rely entirely on dead reckoning. This was far from satisfactory, but I hoped that after five months of judging winds and drifts, my skill would prove equal to the task. As a matter of fact, if my reckoning was correct, I had gone through already—and with the feeling that I was now in a relatively narrow patch of sea, surrounded all about the card by golden-beached palm-greened islands, my spirits rose to a pitch of elated frenzy. However, from now on I would have to be very careful, as I was steering blindly through some of the most dangerous navigable waters in the world. Admitted, *Britannia* was not a big ship, a yacht even, but . . .

June 25   *156th day*
I hope I am on course. Haven't seen any land, but it must be near. Feeling a bit wary about the Hogsty Reefs. Got a sixth sense for this sort of thing, and now something tells me I'm heading straight for them. It would be very bad luck indeed to have come so far only to pile up onto a flipping reef. As I row I cannot see where I am going, and with rain and the noise I make with the oars, it would be almost impossible for me to sight or hear any breakers in time to avoid them. When riding the crest of a wave, Britannia goes

at three knots and over; hitting a rock won't do her any good. Come, Venus; you ought at least to come out—let me have a peep at your lovely body. No chance. I just can't get a sight, not even a single position line. Well, let's trust luck.

June 26   *157th day*
Near dawn and—ye gods! Saw her!—just as she was rising through a hole in the clouds. Horizon unbelievably black and low. How she managed to get through for me to see her I'll never know; but see her I did, for about two minutes, and all during that time she blinked and flashed at me like mad. Planets don't twinkle, so I knew right away there was something wrong somewhere and she was trying to warn me. Stopped rowing at once. Hit by a squall immediately after, and for two hours it was as if the sea and sky had gone mad. Lightning, thunder, rain, and the wind northeast, gusting up to Force 6 and 7. Magnificent spectacle of raw, naked fury! I felt, as never before, as if I were part of it and, deliriously happy, cursed and sang throughout it all, at the top of my voice, while Britannia, frightened out of her wits, screamed bloody rape. I felt full of energy suddenly, and the strength and power of the gods burned like lava in my veins. And I positively itched to grab the oars and row, row, row. But I didn't. My beloved had warned me not to and I heeded her, which probably saved my life.
The squall ended as suddenly as it had begun. And just at the last possible moment before the sun rose, I was able to shoot a couple of stars and fix my position—which turned out to be only five miles northeast of the Hogsty Reefs. Had I rowed, as I wanted to, I would have hit them square, right at the height of the storm. I'm sure Britannia would much have preferred to be raped by the sea rather than by them. As for myself, I'll just have to sacrifice a virgin to my goddess. It's been a long time since I last did, but surely she deserves it now. Trouble is, will I find one?

Arrival: Florida, July 19.

J. F. in the *Britannia,* on arrival.

This, I suppose, was one of those mysterious, inexplicable things that happen so often at sea and turn sailors into superstitious beings. To try and find an explanation for them is quite pointless. For me to attempt to explain my reactions in a reasonable way would be not only most unromantic, but impossible. I simply felt, *knew*, that I had to stop rowing, no matter what, and that Venus—it was Venus, twinkles or no twinkles!—was trying to warn me of the proximity of danger. I heeded her and saved myself. What more is there to be said?

June 27   *158th day*
Fine weather.
Off the Acklins lighthouse; can just about see the reflection of its flashes on the horizon. I am right in the middle of a shipping lane. As I was sleeping during the day, I was awakened by a ship's whistle, and when I scrambled out to see what was going on, I saw the funniest ship in the world, with two big balloonlike contraptions dominating her upper structure. Other than that she had absolutely normal lines, which made it all the more weird. She had stopped, obviously puzzled to see a boat like Britannia *drifting along and no one visible. Waved I did not need anything and, as she pulled away, went back to sleep. I still wonder what those balloons were for.*
Rowed ten hours.

June 28   *159th day*
A Russian ship, coming from Cuba, stopped by and, while I kept rowing, started to lower one of her lifeboats, obviously with the intention of coming to my "rescue." I waved madly that I was all right and did not need anything, but they went on and soon had a lifeboat on the water coming toward me. Told them I was O.K., but they invited me on board, and I decided that since they had gone through all that bother,

it would be just as well if I went. As with the Talsy, my previous Russian ship, the captain of the Krasnozavodsk—I hope
I'm spelling it right!—was in no hurry, and I was invited to
have a shower. They were an extraordinarily nice bunch and
kept insisting that I must surely need something, and to
make them happy, I accepted some water, cigarettes, pine-
apples and canned fruit. Also had a shower and sharpened
my knife.

They were all surprised and a little amazed at what I was
doing and asked me if I would mind having my picture
taken with the whole crew around me. Of course I was delighted to oblige. There was a young, healthy-looking lass
named Svetlana, and I pulled her to my side and gave her a
"from-England-with-love" kiss as they filmed. She was very
happy about it and, to make sure the picture would come
out, asked me to repeat the performance so that the photographers could take more pictures. When I finally left, I was
feeling very happy myself. Russian ships are wonderful.

At night headed for Cay Verde, and for this I had to go
north. Quite a bit off course, but I did not mind.

Right now the wind is coming from the southeast, Force 6,
and a very bad squall with thunder and lightning and so
much rain I cannot see the compass to steer by. It's raging!
I wonder if I'll make the cay after all.

Ten hours rowing today.

June 29   160th day
Land ahoy! By Jupiter! The first since the island of Hierro,
back at the Canary Islands.

Two points off my starboard bow the low shape of a very
small cay was barely visible in the first light of dawn, maybe
three, four miles away. Took as much as four hours to
get there, because I had actually already passed it when
I spotted it and had to row against the wind.

It's a green cay, green all over. A bit of white beach and dots
of rocks all around. Lovely! Anchored in two fathoms, about

a hundred feet from the beach, and went ashore. Seabirds
all over the place, and I spent the day relaxing and trotting
around, feeling great.
In the afternoon I went spearfishing. I just had to find a lob-
ster! In a matter of minutes I caught plenty of grunts, group-
ers, snappers, but my lobster was nowhere in sight. I perse-
vered, but it was not until after three hours of looking around
that I finally spotted one—good size, too, but I'm almost
sure the only one in the surroundings.
Left Cay Verde—hope it's Cay Verde, 'cause I haven't
checked by taking a sight at sunset—and spent the night
thinking how I was going to cook my lobster.
Rowed ten hours.

The sight of Cay Verde, the first land in five months, gave
me immense joy. Once ashore I found I could hardly walk,
my legs felt so wobbly, and after spending the best part of
the morning in feverish exploration, I was so contentedly exhausted that I felt I never wanted to leave the place. The
temptation to spend at least a few days in total relaxation
was overwhelming. As I lay on the beach, luxuriating in the
warm caress of the sand, the sight of *Britannia*, gently bobbing at the end of her anchor line, was most uninviting. She
looked so frail, so puny and dilapidated, that the idea of
crossing the Atlantic in her, of actually living within her con-
fines during the past five months, suddenly hit me as so unbelievable, so preposterous, that I almost cried. Surely it was
not true; it could not have, it had not, happened. It was just
another fantastic dream of mine, from which I would presumably wake up to find myself . . . where but on the sand
of a barren patch of grass and rocks in the middle of nowhere!

I cursed and raved, but it soon became obvious to that
portion of my brain still capable of clear reasoning that I
could not afford luxuries. If only a few hours on dry land had
thrown me into such a state of dejection that, for a fleeting

moment, I even contemplated the idea of sinking *Britannia* then and there rather than go back to the oars, what would two or three days do?

Gradually the joy of my first steps on terra firma was turned into sour, frustrating bitterness by the inescapable need to relinquish what I had thought of as Paradise for my own private Hades. So I left—but not before spending the afternoon diving in the crystalline waters that surrounded the cay.

It is one thing to dive in the open ocean. There all one can see is a glaucous-blue, mysterious void. Every so often a glimpse of real or imaginary shadows will send thrills of excitement, tinged with apprehension, through the most unimaginative swimmer. Nothing that I know can be more disquieting than to follow a big shark till it disappears, leaving one floating over a bottomless gloom without knowing where it is anymore, yet feeling it is there all the time and that, if it cannot see you, it knows of your presence. However, exciting as that can be, it cannot be compared to the ecstatic feeling of gliding with weightless, effortless grace under a forest of corals, in and out of deeply indented ravines, among schools of multicolored fish—always watching, with wary suspicion, ready to dart away at the least brusque movement.

It had been years since my last dive in shallow tropical waters, but I found myself so enthralled by the marvel of it that I soon forgot the passing of time and the reasons by which I happened to be there. It was terribly disappointing to find that my ears no longer would take the pressure below four fathoms, but as the bottom here was seldom deeper than that, I was able to explore a great number of holes and crevices in my search for lobsters. Amazingly, not one was to be found, and soon my hunting instincts were distracted toward more exciting prey.

The first grouper I speared, a five- or six-pounder, was snatched away from me by a huge barracuda. A five-foot barracuda is not an everyday sight, and this, plus the fact that I had not seen her approach, gave me such a surprise that I nearly let go of my gun. After reloading and a careful look around to see if any more unwelcome visitors were hanging about, I decided that a big barra is definitely good sport, and a cheeky one like this sorely needed a lesson.

Popular belief notwithstanding, barracudas are not very dangerous. Nevertheless, they are fearless and just about the meanest-looking fish one can think of. They have enormous, clearly visible canine teeth in equally enormous mouths. To see them continually opening and closing those disproportionate, doglike jaws, as it is their habit to do, while they hover, almost motionless, the silvery, slender body poised to strike in a flash of sudden viciousness at the blink of an eye, can be most unnerving. Furthermore, one knows that if they do decide to attack, there is damn-all one can do about it. In going after the big barracuda on my own I knew I was more than evenly matched, and once more I enjoyed on my skin the pricklish sensation of latent danger that comes from stalking a potentially dangerous animal.

Great barracudas are said to grow up to ten feet long. They might, but the biggest I have ever seen or caught was a six-footer. The present one, at five feet, looked huge (it must be remembered that below water everything looks a third bigger than it really is), and I wanted to make dead sure that my first shot would be the mortal one. To accomplish this, I intended to strike at a particular spot—slightly above her midsection, an inch or so behind the gills. If my aim was true, death would be instantaneous.

Easier said than done! Like most barracudas, she seemed to know the exact limits of a spear gun's range, and in spite of my efforts, she always kept her distance, a maddening foot or two beyond the dangerous circle. Soon it was obvious that this situation called for a different strategy, and I decided to resort to a trick that had seldom failed me in the past. I stopped chasing her, turning my attention toward a tiny school of yellowtail snappers loitering, with seeming lack of concern, round a cluster of coral heads. Within a minute I had one and lost half of it to the barra, even though I was half waiting for it to happen. The bitch was at it like a flash of lightning, a clean bite and away, leaving only the head of the unfortunate yellowtail dangling precariously at the spear's end. This I managed to retrieve, and I held on to it while reloading—then, with a flick of the wrist, threw the bait a mere yard ahead of me. The snapper's head slowly sank, and I kept pace with it—ready, waiting.

Sure enough, the barracuda was not long in coming in. Some instinct must have warned her that this time it would not be so easy. Now she approached ever so slowly, almost haltingly, but nevertheless she came. I followed her with the spear, aiming carefully, tenaciously resisting the temptation to let go till I had her exactly where I wanted her. Ten feet, six, four . . . *Whang!* As the shaft buried itself with a thud, precisely on target, the big barra suddenly stopped as if petrified, and the big, slender body shook in spasms of rigid quivers. Then, after a last, abrupt, convulsive jerk that shook her from head to tail, she seemed to relax and, tilting over, slowly began to sink.

Few things can be compared to the satisfaction of a really perfect shot, and I felt so delighted by it that, forgetting I was underwater, I laughed—with the imaginable result!

Two hours later, I had bagged enough fish to feed a regiment, but not a single lobster. Eventually I got one, and that was that. The time for fun and games was over. Florida was a long way still.

Mostly uninhabited, the extensive chain of islands, cays and reefs that form the Bahamas lies between 20°56′ and 27°25′ North Latitude and 71°00′ and 79°20′ West Longitude. From Cay Verde, at the easternmost fringe of the Great Bahama Bank, I intended to follow a northwesterly course which, with luck, would enable me to reach the western end of the bank at about the same latitude as the tip of Florida. I figured that a hundred and fifty miles would give me enough

leeway to cross the Florida Strait without being swept past
Miami by the two-to-three-knot current generated by the
Gulf Stream.

At the same time, I wanted to give Cuba the widest possible berth. What Cuban patrols might make of *Britannia*, if
spotted, was anybody's guess, but I sure had no inclination to
present myself as target practice for some trigger-happy
zealot. I might have been wrong, of course; but it had been
my sad experience that when my South American friends
turned Communist, their personalities suffered from loss of
even the most elementary sense of humor.

June 30   *161st day*
Cooked my lobster with plenty of fried onions and butter.
What a treat!
Slept all day. Very tired, as I had no rest yesterday.

July 1   *162nd day*
Today I feel full of nostalgia for the old days when I used
to smuggle and fish in the Caribbean. It is a sea full of mem-
ories for me—of danger, romance, the beginning of my ad-
venturous career. When I first arrived, I had been a green-
horn in search of adventure—young and naive, head and
feet in the clouds. When I left five years later, after a non-
stop spree of capers during which I did almost everything
that can be done, I was as broke as I had started but full
of experience, as hard a son of a bitch as there could be—
a man. I have gone soft now compared with then, but per-
haps it is better this way. All the same, they were wonder-
ful days.
Oh well, let us leave the past and look ahead. Nothing but
sky and water. Bloody sea!
Rowed ten hours.

July 2   *163rd day*
Been diving quite a lot today, trying to reach six fathoms.

When I started at Cay Verde, I could not go over four—this when I had prided myself on my prowess as a diver, remembering the days when I could free-dive and catch my fish as deep as ten and thirteen fathoms. Of course, it's been years since then, but all the same I never would have believed I was so far out of condition. It's all to do with my ears: they just won't take the pressure and hurt like hell. Went down as far as five fathoms today; must get at least to six before I leave the bank.
Rowed ten hours.

A look at the chart will show the Great Bahama Bank as an enormous expanse of shallow water, average depth four fathoms, with Andros, the biggest of the Bahama Islands, roughly in the middle. To the south lies Cuba. As far as big ships are concerned, there is only one navigable passage: the Old Bahama Channel, which runs along the Cuban north coast.

From Cay Verde my intention had been to go northwest, but because of wind and currents I had only managed to make good along an easterly course, and now found myself approaching the Cay Lobos lighthouse, at the very edge of the bank. Cuba was less than thirty miles to the south. It looked as if, in spite of all my efforts, the fortunes of my landfall were now entirely at the mercy of a whimsical wind; a northerly breeze and I would find myself pulling Fidel's beard! A privilege I felt strongly inclined to leave in the far more capable hands of freedom-loving Cubans.

Luckily, for the moment these were but speculations. By now I had not the slightest doubt that I would make it to Florida, and if the winds did change, as long as I stayed on the Bank I could always anchor and wait for better luck. My main worry was that of being so near the edge. If, at night, I strayed into the deep channel and the wind changed before I realized what had happened, then I would be in trouble. With this in mind, I decided to take careful soundings every hour.

July 3   *164th day*
Met a couple of fishing boats and had a chat with the guys.
I hope to arrive at Miami by the eleventh, in the morning,
if the weather holds.
Now that I'm practically there, I feel emptied and dissatisfied
with everything. Got the funny notion that the sea didn't
really put up a fight at all, and somehow cheated me out of
it. The gods know I have had a hard job getting here; still,
there is something missing somewhere, and I just can't think
what. Maybe I'm just too bloody tired.
Dived to seven fathoms today, touching bottom. My ears
were whistling like an express train, and the pain was so
brutal I had to close my eyes and bite the snorkel's mouth-
piece almost in half. Came up spitting blood from burst
blood vessels—but that's all right. All the same, it was a
stupid thing to do. I'm a horse's arse, definitely.
Rowed ten hours.

With light winds from the southeast, I had begun to row
due north and, with painful slowness, eventually managed to
see the Cay Lobos lighthouse disappear to the south. It was
hard going, but I was gaining latitude, pulling away from the
specter of Cuba. The fishermen had told me that as long as I
stayed on the Bank, I had little to fear from Cuban patrols;
and so another worry was gradually left behind.

July 4   *165th day*
Felt so tired last night that as I was resting for a spell in my
rowing, I just fell asleep sitting on deck and had another
one of my stupendous dreams. The sea had decided to give
me battle, and I was fighting a most terrifying hurricane.
It went on for three days and nights, and I was definitely
winning when the bitch, in despair, asked Juno, who hates
my guts, to help, and she went to Jupiter asking him a favor,
without saying what, and the doddering old goat, to get rid
of her, said yes. She asked him to strike me down with his

lightning—and having promised, he had no choice but to do so.

Down came a bolt, and with it, the end.

The fallen hero was floating between sea and sky, and another battle, this one for my spoils, raged round me, and although I was dead, I could hear and see it all. No less than mermaids and Valkyries were fighting over me—the mermaids striving to take me down into the abyss, the Valkyries into Valhalla. I prayed for the Valkyries to win, and as I did so, Brünnhilde galloped by and, without stopping, snatched me away, and we went up into the clouds. But although magnificent in her warriorlike beauty, she was ice to the touch, and I suddenly found myself screaming for my beloved, my goddess, my Venus, to come and take me away. Could she beat the formidable rival? Don't know how she managed, but suddenly I found myself in her arms, enveloped in the incredible softness of her body, and she took me to Olympus, where all the gods had gathered to hail and greet me. And we sipped nectar and the nymphs danced and sang for us, and then we made love, and I wished I could happily stay dead forever after.

A cold shower woke me up. Alas, I was alive and miserable, and it was time for me to call London.

As I lifted the aerial, lightning flashed, and looking up, I could have sworn I saw Juno looking down on me, her face distorted in a wicked grin. The dark finger of the aerial was already pointing to the sky, the only high thing for miles, and what a temptation it must have been for Jupiter! So I got it down as fast as I could and, cringing like a little mouse, hid myself in my hole, deciding that London could go to hell for a while. After all, I had nothing really important to report.

What the hell is wrong with me? Am I cracking up like an old woman? By all the gods, if I get it, I know what it will be like now. What more could a mortal man ask?

I finally made the call—but, honestly, I have seldom known

what it is like to be afraid as I did for as long as that call went on, and I sweated and sweated as I can remember doing only once before—and that was when I had a sauna bath to see what it was like.

Does anyone think I should have my dreams psychoanalyzed?

13

July 5   166th day
Couldn't dive more than three fathoms today—my ears are still sore.

Nothing happened. Hot, tired. Come on, Florida, move a bit toward me or I feel as if I'll never make it! These last days are the worst. I get tired so easily now. I'm definitely not fit anymore.

Must try to see if I can get John Austin and Martin Cowling to come and meet me on the seventh. That way I will be able to leave the Bank and get into the Strait, where the current should help me a lot. At least I'll be drifting north, whereas now I have easterly winds and it is very hard to row north, as I'm doing.

Ten hours today.

I was now in radio contact with London almost every day. Apparently interviewers, photographers and reporters, together with John Austin and Martin Cowling, had flown to Florida a few days before and were organizing my reception. As the end drew near, both ITN and the *Daily Sketch* were getting anxious. Under the terms of our contract, I had promised them an exclusive interview to be held at sea. This, I decided, would be possible only if I stayed on the Bank. The idea was for me to get as near the western edge as I could, anchor, then radio my position, enabling them to find me with a yacht they were chartering in Miami. In principle I had nothing against this, but I wanted to get it over as soon as I could.

July 6   *167th day*
Told London I would like to be met by John Austin, Martin Cowling and company the morning of the eighth—that is, two days from now. I hope they can do it. I am finding it very hard going to keep on the Bank. Spent the whole day at anchor. Naturally, I want to get going, and the current is favorable. Once in the Florida Strait I ought to go like a shot, and fooling around with this anchor business to stay on the Bank is time-consuming and does nothing to improve my temper.
A plane with a lot of photographers flew over me for about twenty minutes during the afternoon, so although I have heard no news on the radio, I guess they know by now that I'm about to arrive.
Think I have hurt my left ear, as I find it impossible to dive under four fathoms yet; the right one clears all right.
Rowed ten hours.

According to London, it seemed there had been some trouble in chartering a suitable boat. Because of technical problems with the radio (I had the right crystals but the

wrong aerial), I could communicate with Miami only by re-
laying my messages through London. Thanks to the astound-
ing range of my Marconi radio—over five thousand nautical
miles if conditions were right—this was not difficult, but it
was time-consuming and open to confusion. As it happened,
they insisted on having a look at me from the air, so to facili-
tate the search, I had given my position and lost most of the
day anchored. The way it turned out, somebody had goofed
and they had looked for me in the wrong place. Nobody
knew who had chartered the plane I had seen, nor how they
learned where I was. Total confusion seemed to reign, and I
was asked to report my new position in the morning so that
they could try again.

July 7   *168th day*
This is good. The Daily Sketch *and ITN will meet me tomorrow. I hope everything goes O.K. I'm fed up. Happily,
all will be over soon, but now the hours seem to drag forever.*
*Spent the day at anchor again, as I made a stupid mistake
and did not get my position right this morning. Not knowing
where I am, I dare not drift. Heard on WGBS Miami a radio
news bulletin that I was about to arrive and that the Coast
Guard had said that my sighting yesterday, some one hundred and fifty miles northeast of Miami, was consistent with
the positions reported by several ships that had spotted me
during the past weeks. What a cheek—consistent indeed!*

Because of an error in reading the sextant at dawn, I could
not be sure of my position; after that it had been overcast
most of the day, and I had been unable to correct the sight.
The wind being from the south, I was once more forced to
anchor, to prevent *Britannia* from drifting too far north.
A new fix at dusk proved it had been a wise decision,
as I was right at the edge of the Bank, on 23°47′ North Lati-

tude. From here I would have to enter the Gulf Stream right away, for if I went farther north along the Bank, I would never be able to make it across without being swept way past Miami. All I could do was sit tight, hoping the ITN yacht would find me the following day. Once the blessed interview was over and done with, nothing could stop me. In the Gulf Stream I hoped to average sixty miles a day. Two days and I would be there. Two God-damned days was all! Why was I waiting here?

July 8   *169th day*
London said the boat broke down at sea—so they won't come today. Another day lost!
Very hot.
Swam around most of the time, but there are no fish. The muscles of my whole body are getting stiff and I feel sore—I guess because of inactivity, which is why I am swimming. Can't dive over three fathoms yet. Pity, but anyway, the bottom here is only four fathoms.
Beautiful night.

Another reason for swimming was that I was fuming, but there was nothing I could do about it. A promise is a promise, and like it or not, I intended to keep it. Meanwhile, I tried to make the most of the situation. I spent the day swimming, the night relaxing—but it was not easy. Granted, not having to row was a relief; but aside from that, I felt restless and fidgety. The sudden disruption of six months of hard, self-imposed routine had left me in a perilous state of unbalance. To stop short of my goal when I was practically there—for a television interview in the middle of nowhere!—was lunacy. I felt as if all my vital energy, every ounce of which had been deployed to the utmost, had begun to revert on itself with frightening swiftness. As a result, I was in serious danger of losing my sense of reality in a miasma of complacency. After all I had gone through, the task of rowing *Britannia* across the Gulf Stream appeared deceptively easy; but until I actually beached her on Florida's sands, I was not done. A hundred things could happen still: a sudden storm; a collision; a stupid accident, like breaking an arm or a leg at the last moment—anything could happen, anything!

I had promised, and I would wait, but only for another day. No more.

July 9   *170th day*
Still at anchor, waiting. This is terrible, to be so near and to sit on my arse like this instead of going on. I'm not there yet and I'm allowing myself to relax as if my journey were at an end. And this is wrong, wrong! I still have a dangerous, difficult stretch to cover, one hundred and forty miles, and I am just asking for trouble by not pushing on. Why the hell don't they come?
Seaplane overflew me during the afternoon. ITN has at last found me. Dropped a pack with my pipe tobacco and a note saying they could not land because it was too rough—this when there is not a whisper of wind and the sea is like a mirror. That pilot must be out of his mind, and a lousy navigator to boot—giving my position as 24°10′ North, 79°30′ West. Didn't even bother to look at the chart to know it was wrong, by forty miles at least, as that would put me in the middle of the Stream, in four hundred fathoms of water. Apart from the fact that I am obviously anchored, I cannot be so far wrong in my own estimate, which makes my position 23°47′ North, 79°05′ West.
Anyway, another seaplane with two photographers arrived and landed an hour later. Pilot said he had never seen the water so smooth. Was not sure of position, but said he would check and inform the other. ITN asked me to wait for them until tomorrow at sunset, as they will try to find me with a boat. Against all my better judgment, I'll wait, but I'm definitely not staying around here a moment longer than that.

Look after me please, Venus—don't let me relax too much, please.

July 10   *171st day*
By midafternoon, as I was beginning to give up hope, they finally got here in a beautiful yacht, the Costa Grande. *Martin was with them, and it was really great to see him again. Had a ball and got sloshed. Tremendous meal, with big, juicy steak. Marvelous!*
All over now, on my way again, but I feel very bad. What I feared has happened: I have let my defenses down. I was so happy to see them that I could not resist the temptation and committed the unpardonable stupidity of getting drunk. My self-discipline is gone, and I don't know how I am going to make it now. The skipper of the Costa Grande *had offered me a tow, and I'm beginning to think I should have accepted; but how could I, after struggling so much, for so long, to get here on my own?*
Rowed only four hours. Feel dead. Kept falling overboard during the night. Still under the effects of the whiskey and the euphoria of the meeting. I am really a fool.

Recriminations after the fact always come easy. What was the use! I knew what I shouldn't do, yet I went ahead and did it. I could not resist the temptation. As simple as that.

July 11   *172nd day*
Rowed due west in the hope of making good a northwesterly course. But now I find myself at the edge of the Cay Sal Bank, slightly south of my position in the Great Bahama Bank. So either there was no current whatsoever, or something went wrong. If so, what?
Terribly hot; no wind or clouds. The sun is baking me alive, and I feel weaker than a baby. Could not sleep at all.
My position decided me to go up due north tonight.

Rowed very little, only six hours. What the hell has happened to me?

The skipper of the *Costa Grande* had suggested I row due west, instead of northwest as had been my intention, or the Gulf Stream would push me on past Miami. At first I was reluctant to follow his advice. My own judgment that I could —in fact, should—row northwest was based on a meticulous study of the charts and, by then, an absolute knowledge of *Britannia's* and my own capabilities. The approximate axis— that is to say, the area where the current of the Gulf Stream is at its strongest—runs almost parallel to, and about twenty miles off, the eastern tip of Florida's peninsula, a full hundred miles due west of my own position on the edge of the Great Bahama Bank, at 23°47′ North Latitude. Once I pushed off the bank I would enter not the Florida Strait proper, but the Santaren Channel, which runs between the Great Bahama and another bank, the Cay Sal. In my opinion, especially in the absence of wind, the influence of tides clashing with the Gulf Stream over the Cay Sal Bank might produce a strong countercurrent running south along the Santaren Channel. However, I was not sure and did not know these waters, and allowed myself to be persuaded. To row west rather than northwest did not seem as if it would make all that difference anyway.

So I headed west. As it happened, owing to the disconcerting way the compass kept jumping out of focus—that needle seemed to point all over the card at the same time!—the course I actually *did* follow will forever remain a mystery.

July 12   *173rd day*
Couldn't believe my eyes this morning as I fixed my position: 23°22′ North, 79°22′ West. Thirty miles southwest of where I had been on the Bank! This after rowing north for most of the night. Where is the current that was supposed to take me past Miami if I wasn't careful?

Not been able to sleep at all since leaving the Bank. Tired as never before. Cannot think. The day incredibly hot—95° Fahrenheit; no wind. The sun is cooking me alive, and I should have been in Miami already. I could shoot myself. My fault, of course, and no one is to blame but myself. If I could only get some sleep! It's like a desert out here. If there were sand around me instead of water it would make no difference.

I find rowing for more than one hour impossible, and this at night. Have I got no willpower left? By Jupiter, am I going to throw in the towel now, when I'm practically there? I cried victory too soon and now must pay the price of my own foolishness. Must row, get up and row, row.

July 13   *174th day*
Went up again, about ten miles from where I started, only I am in the Santaren Channel instead of on the Great Bahama Bank.
The day is oppressively hot; not a breath of wind. Have diarrhea and feeling terribly bad in general. Cannot sleep— too hot, and perhaps I'm too tired for it.
And I don't understand at all what's going on in these waters. As it is, I have traveled in a circle; what now?

It is not at all easy to describe what I was going through. After the euphoria of my meeting with Martin Cowling and all those photographers and reporters, taking pictures and interviewing, each outdoing the others in fussing over me, making me feel and—what is worse—believe that I was the greatest man ever to go to sea, I had been thrown back into my own cramped little world—bewildered, sick and now thoroughly dejected at the way things were going.

Three days during which I had been not only unable to sleep, but so sick to the stomach that if I was not squatting over the side, I was vomiting.

Without wind or clouds, the heat was torrid, the sun an

incandescent blaze. To think or concentrate on a problem became increasingly difficult. Mostly I moved around doing things out of habit and self-preservation. I suppose that after six months, all the do's and don'ts of staying alive in the tiny, bobbing world of *Britannia* had been so ingrained into my subconscious that I would go mad and still perform the necessary chores. To make matters worse, I was unable to communicate with London, having run out of petrol for the generator. The batteries had been drained of energy during the last call, the day before my rendezvous with the *Costa Grande*. It had been arranged that Martin would look for me on the eleventh with an airplane and drop a gallon or two. According to news bulletins I picked up on my transistor, he had tried to several times in the past three days. He had looked where I was *supposed* to be, and speculation as to my whereabouts and safety was beginning to mount. After all, I was supposed to have reached Miami in two days. How could anyone guess that on the morning of the thirteenth I was but ten miles from my position on the tenth? I would dearly have liked to know the answer to that one myself. How could it have happened?

July 14   *175th day*
Again today I got the surprise of my life. This is really yesterday, at sunset, but as I go by GMT, it's the fourteenth. The fact is that during the daylight hours of the thirteenth, I have drifted forty miles south. How could that be possible? There was no wind, and the water seemed absolutely dead. Am I going nuts? I can't believe it, but after checking and rechecking, I have to admit the facts. What the hell—am I going to circle round all over again?
Still have diarrhea; getting to feel really weak, and morale very low. The only thing that keeps me going is a shred of willpower left over from somewhere. I must get to Miami under my own steam. I'll bloody well sink Britannia *and go*

down with her before submitting to the indignity of a tow.
So help me, I'm going to make it!

Baffling, incredible, but there was no escaping it, I was
going round and round, up and down like a yo-yo, in—most
mystifying of all—a sea so calm that even the Serpentine on
a windy day was rough by comparison. Also, I was getting
dangerously near to Cuba again—far too near for comfort.
There was no doubt now that *Britannia* was in the grip of a
southerly current, whose strength fluctuated wildly but
which was, nevertheless, unmistakably real. But that it was
so powerful as to make us drift forty miles in twelve hours
was hard to believe, and I refused to accept it. Far more
credible was that on the morning of the thirteenth I had
made a navigational error. For one thing, I had based my assumption on a two-star fix, the absolute minimum under
the best circumstances.

A sight taken from a rowboat whose deck is practically
level with the sea can never be as accurate as one taken from
the bridge of a big ship—in fact, stability and visible horizon
vary so enormously that the two cannot be compared. Still,
navigation, as an exact science, is left behind in the class-
room; at sea it becomes an art, and so it is called The Art of
Navigation. Those who have tried to make star and horizon
meet in a Force 8 gale while clutching the mast of a ten-
tonner for dear life will know what I mean. Now, as a navigator I'm strictly average, but like most navigators with a lot of
practice in all kinds of weather, I know by instinct whether a
sight taken under unfavorable conditions can be relied upon
or not. At dawn on the thirteenth, visibility had been perfect,
the sea glassy. Normally I should have pinpointed *Britannia's* position to within a mile. If I had made a mistake, how
gross could it be? Ten, fifteen miles—surely not more than
twenty? Even so, to make me drift twenty miles in twelve
hours, it has got to be some current! Why, at this rate *Britan-*

nia would be kissing Cuban soil in less than thirty hours!
Luckily, I was beginning to feel much better, and after a
hearty dinner, some measure of strength seemed to flow back
into my limbs.

July 15   *176th day*
Did thirty miles, but without gaining latitude. Went up dur-
ing the night, northwest, and then, when I stopped rowing
at noon, came down again, southwest. Gained longitude only
—but maybe I got out of the bad spot.
I am now twenty miles off Cuba. If the drift south doesn't
stop, Fidel will hear from us.
Battery's too low; just can't make contact with Miami. Wisp
of wind tonight from the southeast; maybe this will help by
stopping drift. This looks like the Canary Islands all over
again, only in reverse—and if we beat that, we're bloody
well going to beat this one. Diarrhea stopped—about time.
Got some sleep, too: not much, but feel better. Ship nearly
ran us down. That's all I need!

In Florida, speculation as to my whereabouts was rampant. To listen without being able to reply was most frustrating. From what I could gather, out of the confusion there
seemed to emerge the general idea that I had been captured
by Cuban patrols and was enjoying the benefits of Castro's
hospitality. In fact, to prevent this, in spite of the temperature I went on rowing most of the day in the general direction of the Cay Sal Bank. Once there, I hoped, if worse came
to worst and wind and current turned against us, I would at
least be able to anchor.

It was backbreaking, truly hellish going, but I was determined not to give in, and to go on fighting to the very end of
my already exhausted reserves of energy. Shortly after
nightfall, a big ship nearly ran us down. Unaccountably, I
had been deaf to the rumble of her engines and props until

suddenly, when I did hear it, it sounded as if an express train were bearing down on us, making me jump out of my seat, panic-stricken and dumbfounded.

Not even in the wildest dream can one imagine how incredibly ponderous a ship's bows can look when seen from a rowboat, at night, fifty yards away and plowing forward with the inexorable finality of a head-on, absolutely unavoidable collision course. There was no time to do anything. I just grabbed *Britannia* and held on to her for dear life.

What saved us was the bow wave and the fortuitous circumstance that *Britannia* was lying not broadside but head-on, a shade off-center to the monster's starboard bow. A split second before the mountain of steel touched us, we were pushed aside like a matchstick by the huge mass of water displaced. Under its impact, *Britannia* reared as if she were about to jump out of the water, then rode down the slope, swirling, swamped—but safe. Once more her extraordinary stability had prevented a capsize. In a few seconds that dark, metallic, awesome shape of death had pushed by, and all was as silent and tranquil as before. By the time the ship's navigation lights flickered in the distance, only the thumping of my heart, and the utter shambles on *Britannia's* deck, were left to bear witness that once more disaster had passed by, leaving us unscathed.

The sky had seldom looked so beautiful, or the stars so bright, as they did when I blew a fervent kiss to Venus. For if there ever was a mortal who had made her work the most overtime, surely I could claim the privilege?

July 16   *177th day*
I'm beginning to breathe again! Apparently we have finally managed to pull out of the trap.
All night, helped by southeasterly winds, Force 3–4, we have been going sweetly, and morning finds us at Elbow Cay, one hundred and twenty miles from Miami. All we have to do

*now is cross the Gulf Stream—and I think our position for
doing so is about as good as any I could wish for.*

*A Coast Guard seaplane flew very low over us as we were
about to cross between the rocky shores of two cays and go
out into the Gulf Stream.*

*Later, during the afternoon, Martin Cowling found us with
a plane and dropped some petrol and goodies. Recharged the
batteries and told him expected to arrive at Fowey Rocks
lighthouse sometime between the nineteenth and twentieth.
I find it hard to believe that soon I'll be ashore. Florida at
last! Who can stop me now?*

It was a day full of surprises. First, the tall, beckoning finger of Elbow Cay's abandoned lighthouse, greeting me
cheerfully in the vaporous light of dawn. I could hardly believe that we had made such excellent progress, but when I
worked out the results of sights taken an hour previously,
they left no doubt. Then came the Coast Guard seaplane,
flying very low, wing tips waggling in salute, as I raised the
oars above my head, crossing them in the sign of victory,
mainly to show I was all right and needed no help.

A few hours later, in the afternoon, Martin's plane, a beautiful Aero Commander, buzzed around like an excited bee. It
dropped five or six packages, of which I was able to recover
only two—or rather, one and a half—as they burst on impact, spilling half their contents over an increasingly widen-
ing area. I managed to grab a few things, but mostly they
either sank or floated away, and I soon gave up the chase.
The last held a hastily scrawled letter from Sylvia saying,
among other things, that she hoped I would enjoy the bananas (half a dozen of which she had put in every parcel)
and other delicacies. It was terribly sweet of her—but only a
woman could think of putting ripe bananas in a pack to be
dropped at sea from an airborne plane! Everything, and I
mean everything, in the polythene bag I had recovered had
to be extricated from a whitish, gluey mess of banana, con-

densed milk, pipe tobacco, broken bits of glass and—God almighty!—suntan oil! But it was wonderful, incredibly wonderful, all the same.

Batteries charged, the radio sparked to life again, and I was asked, via London (for I still could not communicate with Miami), to make for the Fowey Rocks lighthouse if possible. My intention had been to land anywhere in Florida. I had had my fill of fooling around, and said so. But they insisted, and I was too happy to argue and eventually agreed. They also asked me to listen to the news bulletins of WGBS, a Miami station, on my transistor. If there were any important messages, they had the station's cooperation to relay them.

July 17   *178th day*
Here we go again! WGBS Miami keeps broadcasting a message for me saying that I should try to make Fort Lauderdale instead of Fowey Rocks as agreed. Damn it all!—they want me to go for a bloody cruise of the Florida coast! How can they go on asking me to do such things after all I have been through? Must keep my temper. O.K.—Fort Lauderdale it is.

We were riding the axis of the Gulf Stream now and, with the help of a light southeasterly wind, going at, for us, an exhilarating speed.

July 18   *179th day*
After a normal day, at night a squall hit us. Rain poured down as it used to do in the old times, and the wind came from the northwest, Force 5–6, for nearly two hours before going back to southeast. A tanker passed a few yards from us without seeing my flashlight signals—the sea seems determined to pull a few dirty tricks out of her sleeve as a final attempt to beat us.

What a night! With the horizon glowing with what could have only been the reflection of a big city, my spirits soaring with unbridled enthusiasm, I was pulling at the oars with newly found energy—when it happened. The wind faltered—wavering uncertainly, first to the east, then to the southwest, until, unexpectedly, it died altogether. I looked around with apprehension. The splendid glow in the northwest had all but disappeared under the darkest, meanest, lowest formation of clouds that ever sailed the sky. A mighty phalanx of malevolence, it rolled on as lightning goaded it into a thundering frenzy.

It came from the northwest—of all places, from the northwest! What in the name of a thousand gods had I done to deserve this? Were they trying to push me back into the sea? Defeat me when I was but hours from victory?

The frustration of seeing my prize about to be snatched away at the very last moment was so intolerably bitter that, suddenly, one hundred and eighty days of pent-up fears and emotions exploded in my mind, and I went berserk. Possessed by almost demoniacal fury, I grabbed the oars and rowed, rowed as I had never rowed before, raving like a lunatic, swearing that I would crush the sea if she was unwilling to submit to my conquest.

Indifferent to all, the wind blew, and the rain poured down in such solid cataracts I could not see beyond my feet, while the sea toyed with *Britannia*. After an hour or so, my body and soul completely spent by the futility of my efforts, the oars slipped away from my hands and I fell backward. Without even the strength to raise my head, I closed my eyes and cried.

Eventually, somewhat recovered, I managed to get back on my feet, shivering with cold and exhaustion, just in time to see, blinking nervously through the semisolid screen of rain, the green and red lights of a ship. Green and red. I blinked back, until finally the significance of it dawned on me: collision course! With visibility almost nil it was hard, if not impossible, to judge with accuracy her line of approach. All right: if they miss, they miss; if not—hell take them all! I was really and truly past caring.

Nevertheless, at sea one does not survive by doing things according to one's mood, and getting out the torch with a weary sigh, I pointed it toward their bridge. It was a powerful torch, eighty thousand candlepower, and I could hardly believe that if I could see their lights, they could fail to spot the dazzling cone of mine as it sliced a quivering path along luminous raindrops, far into the night.

They did fail.

A big tanker, at least fifty thousand tons of it, blindly pushing on through a squall with visibility reduced to a few hundred yards, in a shipping lane, off a major port—and no one keeping a proper lookout on the bridge! Presumably, they were on automatic pilot and the Officer of the Watch had his eyes glued to the radar screen. If so, I wonder what he made of us! In the end they missed us, but passed so near I could have spat at them.

After two hours, the squall ended as abruptly as it had begun. By then I had resigned myself to being pushed back into the middle of the Strait to ride the Gulf Stream forevermore. However, with the end of the squall, the sky cleared; the glow of Miami—it had to be Miami—was still there, as friendly as ever, and the wind, after dying, blew again from the southeast. Had the sea given up, at last? Whatever the answer, I was in no condition to take advantage of it. The emotional and physical stresses of the last days had taken their toll. My frantic exertions during the squall were the coup de grâce. I could barely crawl around, let alone row.

I lashed the torch to the gunwale with the beam pointed at the aft blister and crawled into my rathole. It was midnight, local time. I passed out the moment my head touched the deck.

I was haled out of my slumber by somebody calling my name: "John! Hey, John, where are you?"

Took some time before it registered, but then—what on earth? I scrambled out, and there they were: the suntanned, grinning faces of two gentlemen with the strongest American accents I had heard in my life.

"Hi, John. How are you? Here, let's shake your hand. You gotta be crazy, man! Sure you don't need anything? How about a drink? You name it, we got it. How about a tow?— No? Say, you sure you rowed this thing across the Atlantic? In six months? You gotta be kiddin'! Say, you Limeys are the craziest bastards under the sun. I ain't kidding; we got to give it to you—you're nuts!"

That was my reception, my first taste of American hospitality—and, man, did it sound sweet! These two chaps were out fishing, bound for Bimini in a boat half the size of *Britannia,* held together by rust, with an outboard engine half as big as their boat. Talk about nuts—I wouldn't have taken that thing across the Thames!

Anyway, after our last bout, the sea had apparently decided to give in, and lapping *Britannia*'s hull, she had pushed her, while I slept, to the very outskirts of Miami. Less than three miles from where I was chatting with my newly acquired friends, a jagged cluster of tall buildings dotted the skyline.

"That's right, chum—that's Miami. You've made it!"

Indeed I had. What a beautiful sight! A few miles to the north lay Fort Lauderdale, and if I wanted to arrive by noon, it was time for me to get going.

As I grabbed the oars, my two friends yelled a farewell and, starting that monstrous engine, roared away, doing at least thirty knots. The sea was in a flat calm, but the sight of that battered, tiny excuse for a boat skimming the water in a cloud of spray, occasionally jumping up and down with fearsome thuds, caused me to shut my eyes in apprehension. One more thump and that thing was bound to disintegrate!

It didn't and soon disappeared into the distance, leaving me with the conviction that Americans were wonderfully stark, raving mad.

By noon I was surrounded by a motley collection of yachts: sloops, ketches, power cruisers and, finally, a big, beautiful charterboat, the *Dragon Lady*, with my reception committee. Everybody was there: my adorable Sylvia; Martin and Morag, his wife; Austin; reporters and photographers.

Since I was only half a mile from the beach, I pulled alongside and asked to be towed in. It was hot; I was tired and practically dying to lie down in a soft, comfortable bed. In my mind there was absolutely no need to go on, and yet, amidst cheers and catcalls, they refused to give me a tow! After I had rowed four thousand five hundred miles, for six months, they insisted I row the last half mile, to actually beach *Britannia* on my own! My comment—the only printable one, that is!—was reported the next day all over the press: "Bloody stupid."

Eventually, I did row myself ashore, and that was the hardest, longest, most irritating half mile I had rowed in my life.

July 19   *180th day*
At 1:45 P.M., *local time*, Britannia *touched the beach, and Sylvia was in my arms, and boats swarmed around, and by all the gods, even the old* Queen Elizabeth *blew the whistle for us, and I almost cried. Hail* Britannia, *we have conquered, and Florida is, at last, ours.*

Our reception was magnificent, and—oh, I love America, love everybody today, but mere words cannot express my feeling, and I will not try. Only one thing I can say, and this to you, my lovely little Britannia: *"I salute you."*

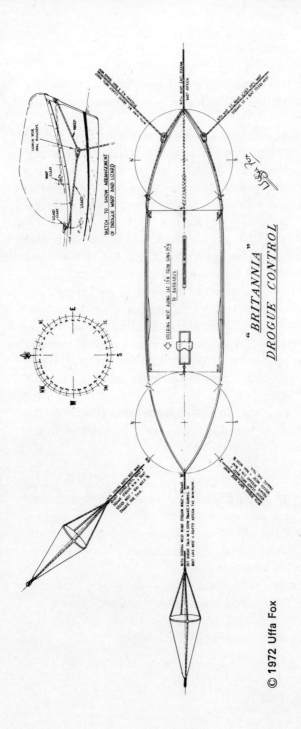

© 1972 Uffa Fox

A ship at sea should always head for the haven where she would be. When heavy weather caused "Britannia" to stream her drogue she could still be steered near her course by adjusting the lizard on the drogue warp, whether streamed ahead or astern.

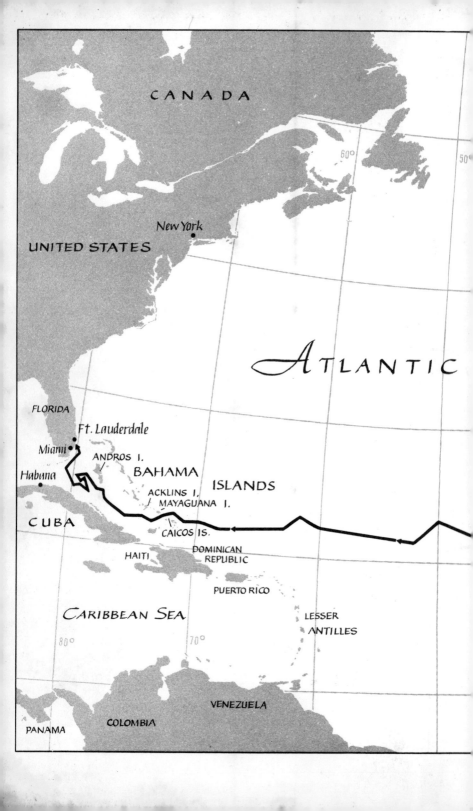